PATHWAY

to our

HEARTS

Archbishop Collins combines two rare gifts: a vivid, engaging style and a deep understanding of Scripture. This book is a marvelous introduction to the ancient Christian tradition of *Lectio Divina* (sacred reading), and a real treasure for meditation on the Word of God. For any Christian longing for a deeper experience of prayer, the author opens the door to a richer daily life rooted in the Sermon on the Mount.

Most Reverend Charles J. Chaput, O.F.M. Cap.
Archbishop of Denver

The recent Synod on the Word of God emphasized the importance of *Lectio Divina*, in deepening our spiritual lives. Archbishop Collins's book, *Pathway to Our Hearts*, is exactly what is needed to make this important approach to praying the scriptures something accessible to all. Archbishop Collins's knowledge and love of the scriptures comes alive in this book.

Most Reverend Gerald F. Kicanas
Bishop of Tucson

The *Lectio Divina* reflections of Archbishop Thomas Collins are the fruit of a shepherd who lives in the House of the Word. I highly recommend these clear, accessible, and hopeful reflections that offer tremendous assistance to all who wish to give flesh to the Word in their daily lives.

Fr. Thomas Rosica, C.S.B.
CEO
Salt and Light Catholic Media Foundation

Through the ancient Christian tradition of *Lectio Divina*, Archbishop Collins deftly, concretely, and pastorally gives us a path in our day to encounter the living God through his holy and transforming Word.

Msgr. Peter J. Vaghi
Author of *The Sacraments We Celebrate*

Archbishop Collins has offered a gift to us. This book on *Lectio Divina* provides not only a method, but an example. If Jesus would come to our diocese and teach us today he probably would use the text of the Beatitudes, as it is a rich, divine study into the new covenant. Not only is Archbishop Collins qualified as a scholar from his many years at Biblicum and the Gregorian University, but he also speaks with authority as someone who has encountered God through his daily practice.

Sr. Meg Funk, O.S.B.
Author of *Lectio Matters: Before the Burning Bush*

PATHWAY
to our
HEARTS

A Simple
Approach to
Lectio Divina
with the
Sermon
on the Mount

ARCHBISHOP THOMAS COLLINS

ave maria press AmP notre dame, indiana

Founded in 1865, Ave Maria Press is a ministry of the Indiana Province of Holy Cross.

www.avemariapress.com

ISBN-10 1-59471-265-4   ISBN-13 (EAN): 978-1-59471-265-4

Cover image © imagebroker / Alamy.

Cover and text design by John R. Carson.

Printed and bound in the United States of America.

Library of Congress Cataloging-in-Publication Data
Collins, Thomas, 1947-
  Pathway to our hearts : a simple approach to lectio divina with the Sermon on the mount / Thomas Collins.
    p. cm.
  Includes bibliographical references and index.
  ISBN-13: 978-1-59471-265-4 (pbk. : alk. paper)
  ISBN-10: 1-59471-265-4 (pbk. : alk. paper)
  1. Sermon on the mount--Meditations. 2. Spiritual exercises. I. Title.
  BT380.3.C65 2011
  226.9'06--dc22
                    2010044271

Contents

INTRODUCTION

Welcome to a celebration of lectio divina.

Lectio divina is a Latin phrase meaning "divine reading" or "sacred reading." It refers to an ancient way of reading the Bible that over the centuries has taken a number of different forms within the tradition of the Church. Lectio divina is one of those terms that is both attractive and vague. Everyone agrees that it is a good thing, but there is some discussion concerning precisely what the term means. Fortunately, there is no copyright on "lectio divina," and all kinds of people can fruitfully engage in something that they describe as lectio divina, and use a rich array of diverse methods, without worrying about getting it wrong or breaking any rules. I should, however, at the start, define what I mean by lectio divina. I trust that this is consistent with what the term means in Catholic tradition, as I have sought to understand it, though I would not presume to claim that my way of doing lectio divina in a public forum is in any way normative.

I think that fundamentally lectio divina is a prayerful encounter with the word of God. By the "word of God," I do not mean simply the text of the Bible; I also mean Christ, our Lord. He is the Word of God. One of the most powerful ways that we encounter him is through the words of sacred scripture. The Word became flesh and dwelt amongst us in Jesus Christ our Lord; so too in a different way, the word becomes flesh and dwells among us in human language, in the divinely inspired texts of scripture. That is why when we read the Bible in lectio divina, when we read the written text of the word of God, we do not simply study it, master it, or try to understand it. In our prayerful reading of the Bible, we are actually encountering the Lord God: we pray that the Holy Spirit will enlighten us so that we may be attentive disciples of Jesus and do the will of the heavenly Father.

Many people have encountered the Lord God through scripture. A famous spiritual writer, Anthony Bloom, had such an experience and describes it in his book *Beginning to Pray* (Paulist, 1970). He explains that when he was young, he was antagonistic to faith, but decided to read one of the gospels to see if his negative views were verified. He picked the shortest gospel, the Gospel of Mark, so as not to waste time unnecessarily in his final look at Christianity. He writes: "When I was reading the beginning of St. Mark's Gospel, before I reached the third chapter, I suddenly became aware that on the other side of my desk there was a presence. And the certainty was so strong that it was Christ standing there that it has never left me." Bloom, an unwilling young man, encountered Christ though the words of the gospel. Similarly, the regular practice of lectio divina may lead willing disciples of Jesus to deepen their encounter with Christ. That is lectio divina. That is divine reading, sacred reading, where we enter into the presence of God through the reading of a biblical passage.

The spirit of lectio divina should shape our response to the Lord in the other occasions in which we read the sacred scriptures, whether it be in Bible study (*exegesis*), or in private reading of the Bible, or in reading the Bible in preparation for teaching or preaching, or in liturgical reading. Our most significant experience of the word of God is in the celebration of the sacred liturgy. When we come together as the people of God gathered around the table of the word and the table of the Eucharist, we encounter Christ in the most intense way possible during our earthly journey. But routine can blind us to his presence. The personal practice of lectio divina, especially when we use the daily lectionary texts, is a most excellent way of preparing for the celebration of the Holy Eucharist, and in particular for being truly attentive to the Liturgy of the Word.

Lectio divina may be experienced in a public setting when many people come together to hear a portion of the Bible read aloud, verse by verse, with periods of silence to ponder the sacred words. Or lectio divina may be experienced in a private setting, when an individual reads a passage of the Bible as an element of personal prayer.

For over ten years I have been leading public sessions of lectio divina. When I became Archbishop of Edmonton I decided to invite the faithful to come to the cathedral one Sunday evening a month, for a formal celebration of Vespers, followed by lectio divina. I have substantially followed the same pattern in Toronto. Around May of each year I choose the scriptural texts for the coming year's lectio divina. I find that a passage of about fifteen verses is best for a forty-five minute session. The texts are chosen according to a theme, and I ask the people who attend the sessions to offer suggestions. One year I divided the Sermon on the Mount into nine sections, and those sessions form the content of this book. Another year I focused on ten psalms. In the year of St. Paul, I used ten Pauline texts. One year I chose the scriptural texts underlying the five Luminous Mysteries of the rosary, and then five texts relating to life in the Spirit. One time I chose biblical texts that illustrate the Ten Commandments, and another year we read the parables of Jesus. I have thought of dedicating a year to one small book of the Bible, perhaps the Letter of James.

In the week preceding the lectio divina, I sometimes study the text, but only briefly. If I prepare more thoroughly

I will end up giving a scripture lecture. I have been a scripture professor for many years, and I have nothing against scripture lectures, but that is not lectio divina. One Sunday, I discovered only an hour before walking out into the cathedral that I had prepared the wrong text. I was able to spend the thirty minutes before the lectio reading the correct text in the presence of the Blessed Sacrament, as I always do, and my lack of further preparation did not seem to make much of a difference. Thirty minutes of prayer is usually the only immediate preparation for a public session of lectio divina, and intentionally so. As long as one is attentive to a constant development of remote preparation, year after year, through study and daily prayerful reflection on the scriptures, one may abbreviate the immediate preparation for either preaching or lectio divina.

Once the texts are chosen and the preparation is complete, it is time for the session, which begins in the cathedral at seven in the evening with solemn Vespers. After Vespers, which is finished by seven thirty, I go to the sacristy and remove my vestments before returning to the sanctuary. I do not consider lectio divina in the cathedral to be a solemn liturgical act (such as Vespers), but rather a personal encounter with the word of God, and an occasion for me as bishop to join with my people in an intimate, prayerful experience of meditation. The goal, ultimately, is that each person will do this every day at home.

I stand at the front edge of the sanctuary, all wired up with one portable microphone for the cathedral and another for the television. Sometimes I speak for a moment about the context of the passage. I use my old red copy of the Revised Standard Version, because I believe that the Bible should be read. I make the Sign of the Cross and invite the people to let go of their distractions so as to be attentive to the word of God. I pray the Jesus Prayer, "Lord Jesus Christ, Son of the living God, have mercy on me, a sinner," since our own sinfulness is a barrier to hearing the word of God. I pray the prayer of Samuel, "Speak, Lord; your servant is listening," and also "Come, Holy Spirit, fill the hearts of your faithful," interspersing these prayers with times of silence. After a few minutes I read the whole scriptural passage slowly, and ask the people to consider one thing that God is saying to them personally in that passage. Then I go through the text, section by section. It is like spiritual lasagna: a layer of text, then a layer of my own reflections, ending with a question to consider regarding the personal application of the text. That's followed by a layer of silence, then a layer of text, and so on. To complete the session, I read the whole text again, slowly, and after a period of silence end with the Our Father, the Hail Mary, the Glory Be, and the Sign of the Cross. The whole lectio divina session lasts about forty-five minutes.

At the prayer of consecration during the ordination of a bishop, *The Book of the Gospels* is held over the new bishop's head. I have often thought of that action as signifying a fundamental dimension of the episcopal mission. As a bishop I am sent to preach the Gospel, and to assist those whom I serve to encounter the word of God. By leading sessions of lectio divina in my cathedral, I seek to fulfill my mission. But all Christians are called to encounter God through the inspired text, and it is my hope that the ancient practice of lectio divina will continue to be adapted in fruitful ways. Priests and religious have a special mandate to help others to enter more deeply into the sacred scriptures, and lay people will be strengthened in their mission of evangelizing the secular world through a personal experience of lectio divina.

"Speak, Lord; your servant is listening."

One goal of a public session of lectio divina is to help the participants to engage in the same practice at home. Here are some suggestions for doing that.

One thing that can help us to encounter God in the scriptures is to read the text aloud, and that happens whether lectio divina occurs in a public or a private setting. Of course, this reading aloud is also done at Mass, but we can do it whenever we read the Bible. Never speed-read the word of God (or any really important text), rushing along quickly to extract the meaning. No, the divine reading of the Bible is prayerful, and occurs at a measured pace; it is a matter of savoring the word of God, repeating the word of God, praying the word of God. When we read aloud, we are using our eyes, our mouths, our ears, our mind and memory to prepare a way for the word of God to enter our hearts. We can become so abstract, so virtual; using our bodies to speak aloud and hear the words is a way to become more fully human again, to engage more fully in the text. Even if no one is around, praying out loud is a good thing to do. Just close the doors and pray out loud; read the word of God aloud.

After all, the words upon the page are somewhat like the marks upon a musician's score. When a conductor comes in to an orchestra, he or she might have the symphony score printed on the paper, but the music is not those little marks. The actual music occurs in the creating of the sound. Similarly, the word of God is meant to be proclaimed aloud. When we speak the word of God, we hear it, we touch it, and we sense it; and God speaks to our hearts. That's why, at the public lectio divina that I lead each month at my cathedral, we first have a solemn celebration of Evening Prayer, in which we chant and sing the word of God. This is good in itself, but also a fitting preparation for encountering the

Lord in the reading aloud of a passage of the Bible in lectio divina.

The experience of lectio divina, whether in its private or public form, is intended to be an encounter with God in prayer through the repeated reading aloud of a small passage of the Bible. Repetition is said to be the mother of learning, and it certainly is the mother of prayer. When we read a scripture text again and again, we can go deeper and deeper into an experience of God's presence and encounter the message within the text. Reading a text once, and rushing on to something else, is useless. That same principle is true in other aspects of life: virtue, after all, is a habit of repeated good actions. The life of holiness is woven out of the daily repetition of virtuous acts, in response to the grace of God. So when we prayerfully read the scriptures in lectio divina, we slow down and lovingly repeat aloud verse after verse, pondering each one, and silently reflecting upon it.

Such an approach to scripture has a further advantage: when we repeat a small scriptural passage aloud, again and again, we can more easily memorize it, and carry it with us beyond our time of prayer into the hectic rush of our daily lives. Words on the page are like money in the bank; words in our memory are like cash in the pocket. The daily experience of lectio divina is meant to enrich our whole day of discipleship; memorizing the sacred words can assist in that.

The experience of reading the biblical text within a period of lectio divina, whether in public or private, is preceded and followed by prayer. I believe that the prayer of young Samuel in the Temple is the most appropriate introduction to a period of lectio divina: "Speak, Lord, for your servant is listening" (1 Sm 3:9). In lectio divina we seek not to master or to grasp the sacred text, but rather, prayerfully and silently, to come into the presence of God through it. We seek to be humbly attentive to God's Holy Word, to savor it, and to let it enter into our hearts as much as into our heads, so that it may transform us.

As I've mentioned, lectio divina can be either public or private. Although I have described the way in which, as a bishop, I have conducted public sessions of lectio divina in the cathedral church of my diocese, I am fully aware that private time in lectio divina is more fundamental to our life in Christ. It is my hope as I lead a public session once a month that this experience will encourage the participants to engage privately in lectio divina every day. In a sense, when I am speaking in the presence of hundreds of people in the cathedral, and of many more who participate in lectio divina through viewing a session on the television, the Internet, or a DVD, I am simply "turning up the volume" of my private lectio divina, as an example of the kind of prayer the participants might engage in at home. I hope that it will be beneficial for them to overhear some of my personal response to the inspired words. I am always conscious that the most important parts of a public session of lectio divina are the repeated reading aloud of the scriptural verses and the extended periods of silence. In the silence each person may meditate upon the text while praying, "Speak, Lord; your servant is listening." Each person brings to the encounter with the inspired word his or her own current situation and past history of sin and grace. In so doing, each invites the Lord to speak personally, by name, as in the Temple of old: "Samuel, Samuel!" And the young man replies: "Speak, Lord; your servant is listening."

Let me say a word about what lectio divina, whether public or private, is not. It is not the study of the biblical text. That is *exegesis*, not lectio divina. It is always helpful to study the Bible, for the sacred text comes through human authors and scribes from a time long ago and from a place far away. God expects us to use our minds to discover information about the biblical text, and to learn more about the human situation within which the inspired text took shape. If we have first studied the text, it will help us to pray it, teach it, or preach it. A knowledge of the human context of the scriptures and their structure is certainly important for all who pray them. God gave us our minds, and it is good to study the Law of the Lord. But lectio divina itself is an intimate encounter with the Lord God through the medium of his inspired word in the context of prayer. It is not exegesis, although exegesis is a good remote preparation for it.

A public session of lectio divina in the cathedral church is not a form of teaching or of preaching, although the personal practice of lectio divina is an important foundation for the ministry of both teacher and preacher. I was once asked, "Why don't you have a question and answer period as part of your monthly scriptural catechesis in the cathedral?" I replied that I regularly have such a period when I teach a class, or give a talk, but that public lectio divina is not catechesis but prayer, as much as the solemn Vespers that precedes it. The full, active, conscious participation of those who are present occurs not in some explicit way, such as is found in bible discussion groups or in a question and answer period with a speaker, but rather in the contemplation of the biblical word during the lengthy periods of silence within the format of a public session of lectio divina.

There is some parallel here to the personal engagement of the Christian in the eucharistic liturgy; though sometimes that engagement takes the form of spoken words or of actions, it reaches its most profound level in the silence of the heart. To participate actively, one need not always be talking or doing.

Now, how in practice, does a person do lectio divina? There are many ways to enter into lectio divina. In the public sessions, we start with evening prayer, from the liturgy of the Hours. It sets the lectio within the context of the prayer of the Church. For private lectio, I suggest that you set aside a time when you can be alone. Try to find some physical setting that allows you to get away for a while from the external distractions of life.

As for the internal distractions within the mind, they can never be fully escaped. Don't worry about that, but to get ready, enter into a phase of quieting your heart. We need an off-ramp to decelerate and exit a busy freeway, and we need an off-ramp when we enter into a period of prayer. We bring with us into prayer all of the confusion and static of our lives. That garbled noise can distract us so that we do not hear the Lord God. We bring troubled hearts. I remember somebody once said, "Whenever I pray, my head is like a tree full of monkeys just chattering away." And that's the way it is so often when we pray. In this introductory quiet stage, the first step is to say, "Speak, Lord, for your servant is listening." Our tendency is to pray, "Listen, Lord, for your servant is speaking." But we must resist this urge and be willing to listen. Say, "Come Holy Spirit." Just let go of all those things that are barriers.

Prepare by asking the Lord to make a pathway straight into your heart, so that his word will come to you. It is impossible to hear his gentle voice when your mind is roaring with distractions. Remember Elijah said that he heard the Lord God, not in the thunder and the lightning, but in the gentle breeze? And so too, when we are in the midst of lectio divina, when we're prayerfully reading the word of God—not mastering it or studying it—we must ask the

Lord to speak, and then be willing to listen. We need to be in peace. So that is the first stage.

The second stage is to read the scriptural passage through, slowly. It should just be a brief passage, maybe ten or twenty verses. You can't do more than that with lectio divina, because it should be just a slow chewing of the word of God. I would suggest trying one of the Mass readings of the day—and then when we come to Mass, we do not come to the readings cold, but will have prayerfully encountered the Lord even before we show up. Read the passage through, one verse at a time, silently pausing and pondering each verse. Ask yourself, what does it say to my head to teach me about the Lord, to my heart to draw me to love the Lord, and to my hands to serve the Lord? Head, heart, hands. "Speak, Lord; your servant is listening."

Just slowly go through verse by verse, preferably reading each aloud, following each by periods of silence. Consider what you think about this particular verse, what God is saying to you today through it. Encounter Jesus in whatever way the Lord speaks to your heart. Read the verse again; then go on to the next verse followed by a little silence, a little time to think. Continue through the passage like this, piece by piece. It won't take too long. And then at the end, read the whole of it again, followed by a little silence; and then end with prayers, such as the Our Father, Hail Mary, Glory Be, and the Sign of the Cross.

After this time of prayerful lectio divina, we have to return again to the busy freeway of life. Pray that through the experience of lectio divina, the Lord will illuminate our minds with heavenly wisdom, inflame our hearts with love, and empower us to do something: head, heart, and hands.

How to Use This Book

Each chapter of this book is structured as a full lectio session. I encourage you to set aside an appropriate period of time to enter prayerfully into the passage as it is presented in each chapter. Begin with the suggested prayer and then slowly read the entire passage. Then read the first verse and the meditation that follows. After each meditation observe a time of silence, listening for God's word to you, and apply the passage to your life. Finally, read the verse again. Then continue to the next verse, repeating this process. At the conclusion of the chapter, reread the passage in its entirety and conclude with the Our Father, Hail Mary, and Glory Be.

If praying a whole chapter requires too long a period of time, you may wish to pray with just one or two verses at a time. Always begin by entering into a spirit of prayer. Then slowly read the whole passage (as presented at the beginning of each chapter). After this, read the particular verse that you will reflect on and the meditation that follows. After each meditation, pause and pray silently. Wait on a word from God and try to connect the passage to your life. Then read the verse again. If you wish to continue with the next verse, repeat these steps. When it is time to conclude, reread the passage in its entirety and then conclude with a prayer. The prayers that begin and end each chapter are fitting ways to open and close each session. It is not important how much you read each time; it only matters that each time of lectio divina is unhurried and is begun and ended with prayer. The entire experience of lectio divina is not meant to be educational, but deeply prayerful.

CHAPTER ONE

Matthew 5:1–12

Speak, Lord; your servant is listening.

Come Holy Spirit, fill the hearts of your faithful, and enkindle in us the fire of your love. Send forth your Spirit, and we shall be created, and you shall renew the face of the earth.

Speak, Lord; your servant is listening.

Seeing the crowds, he went up on the mountain, and when he sat down his disciples came to him. And he opened his mouth and taught them, saying: "Blessed are the poor in spirit, for theirs is the kingdom of heaven. Blessed are those who mourn, for they shall be comforted. Blessed are the meek, for they shall inherit the earth. Blessed are those who hunger and thirst for righteousness, for they shall be satisfied. Blessed are the merciful, for they shall obtain mercy. Blessed are the pure in heart, for they shall see God. Blessed are the peacemakers, for they shall be called sons of God. Blessed are those who are persecuted for righteousness' sake, for theirs is the kingdom of heaven. Blessed are you when men revile you and persecute you and utter all kinds of evil against you falsely on my account. Rejoice and be glad, for your reward is great in heaven, for so men persecuted the prophets who were before you."

⌒

Seeing the crowds, he went up on the mountain, and when he sat down his disciples came to him. And he opened his mouth and taught them.

Jesus is always with crowds. Just before this scene in the gospel, he has been with the people, healing the sick. He is not off alone with a few—he is in the midst of us all. Seeing the crowds, the ones he loves, the ones he at one point says are like sheep without a shepherd, he goes up on the mountain—up on *the mountain*, to speak words of power and majesty. This is our Lord speaking in a profound, formal, and majestic way. He goes up on the mountain as Moses went up the mountain to meet the Lord and to bring his people the Ten Commandments. And here Jesus comes, and seeing the crowds, he goes up on the mountain, showing us the way of discipleship, the way to be servants, children of the heavenly Father.

"When he sat down his disciples came to him." They gather around. They are attracted to him. They want to listen to him. "And he opened his mouth and taught them." He speaks to them and to us. "Speak, Lord; your servant is listening." As we hear this introduction to the Sermon on the Mount, we sense the majestic presence of Christ, who speaks to us words that can change our lives. These are not just a few offhand remarks he is going to make. These words are solemn, formal, and proclaimed from the mountain. He sits down and teaches, with his disciples gathered around him. Like the disciples, as we begin to listen to the Sermon on the Mount, we need to have within our hearts a spirit of reverence and adoration for the Lord God whose words are coming to us, the words that are life, light for our path.

How often, when we hear the word of God, do we have that reverence within our hearts? When we are at Mass, do we remember the ideas in the first reading when we're on to the second reading? Can anyone remember the second reading when we are on to the gospel? How often do the words of the Lord go in one ear and out another? And yet this is *the Lord* speaking to us. We must pray that his words will make an impression on our hearts, that he will be invited into our lives. As we begin this experience of the Sermon on the Mount, let us listen to these sacred words, and then within our own hearts commit ourselves always to listen to the word of God with reverence.

I used to go to a monastery for retreats. Whenever the monk would approach the word of God, he would physically bow down before it; then he would read solemnly. Some of us here have had the opportunity to proclaim the gospel and proclaim the readings at Mass. This is a solemn thing to do. These are the words of life, so we need to have that same sense of reverence for the word of God that is shown in these opening words of the Sermon on the Mount.

I remember once I was studying the Hebrew language in Jerusalem, where even the printed words of the scriptures are treated reverently. We had a little Xerox copy of a text of scripture, and a line at the bottom warned: Do not throw this in the garbage. You know how we tend to take our used missalettes and throw them in the trash—so lightly do we consider the paper that records the word of God!

When we hear the word of the Lord at the gospel reading, we make the Sign of the Cross on our forehead that we may know it, on our lips that we may speak it, and on our hearts that we may live it. We must listen intentionally and carefully to the word of God.

In that spirit of reverence, let us listen to these words that begin the Sermon on the Mount, and resolve in our hearts always to be attentive to God's holy word. May we ask forgiveness for the times that we have been speed-reading the word of God, or have simply treated the words lightly.

> *Seeing the crowds, he went up on the mountain,*
> *and when he sat down his disciples came to him.*
> *And he opened his mouth, and taught them.*

༄

> *Blessed are the poor in spirit, for theirs is the*
> *kingdom of heaven.*

Those who are poor in spirit know their need for God and their dependence on him. However much they might have in life, the poor in spirit have their hands out asking the Lord for help. They know that they aren't masters in this world.

"Blessed are the poor in spirit." Blessed are we when we are poor in spirit and do not think we have our hands on the steering wheel of our own life. Let me be a feather on the breath of God. Let that be my prayer—to be poor in spirit. I may be rich or poor in terms of a bank account, but my wealth is not really the point. My dependence on God is the point. A rich person may be generous and attentive and dependent on the Lord, and a poor person may not be. The point is: whatever our material wealth, we must be poor in spirit and dependent on the Lord.

"Blessed are the poor in spirit." To be blessed is to be at peace, to have a spirit of inner serenity. "Blessed are the poor in spirit for theirs is the kingdom of heaven." This is what it's all about: the kingdom of heaven. If we are poor in spirit, then ours is the kingdom of heaven. If we are attentive to the Lord and know our need for God, we don't have to wait for heaven to come to us at the end of our lives. The presence of God with us begins now and continues all the way to the heavenly Jerusalem. If we have that inner peace now, we will be *blessed*. We will have that stillness in the midst of the storm of life.

Ours is the kingdom of heaven. The kingdom of heaven is the fulfillment; it's ahead of us, but it is also in our midst. Unfortunately, we seek it, along with peace and blessedness, in so many false ways. But if we are poor in spirit, attentive to the Lord and knowing our need for God, then that is enough. That is the kingdom of heaven. It isn't rocket science. It's not complicated. On the other hand, it's not easy either. So often we are not poor in spirit; so often we want to take command with our little egos and agendas. Then we are not blessed. We don't experience the kingdom of God. We just experience the kingdom of our own little ego. That's a pretty small kingdom to get caught up in.

"Blessed are the poor in spirit, for theirs is the kingdom of heaven." In our own lives, have we been attentive to the presence of the Lord? Have we said, "Here I am Lord; I come to do your will. Let me be poor in spirit"? Let's ask our Lord Jesus to help us have that disposition of openness, tenderness, and surrender to the will of God.

Blessed are the poor in spirit, for theirs is the kingdom of heaven.

~

Blessed are those who mourn, for they shall be comforted.

We all have occasion to mourn. Grief comes into each of our lives in different ways. And Jesus says, "Blessed are those who mourn." Perhaps sadness comes our way through the death of a person beloved to us. The ones we love will die, as each one of us will die.

"Blessed are those who mourn." Perhaps too, we need to mourn for our own frailty, to grieve our own sinfulness. Just say, "Lord, forgive me for the times that I have been selfish." Perhaps we mourn for our own weakness and struggles, and our inner anxiety, fear, sadness, and depression. So many things can afflict us in this vale of tears that we travel through. Our faith does not tell us that life will be a happy, happy time. "Have a nice day" is not our prayer. The happy face is not our sign. Our sign is the cross of Christ. One great image of our faith is the *pietà*—Our Lady mourning the death of her beloved son. The Lord himself enters into our reality of death and mourning. He did not cling to his equality with God, but emptied himself to come here even to death—death on a cross. Our faith does not take us out of the struggle of this world, but into the heart of it all, into the storm. And yet Christ is in the storm. When the boat is bouncing around and we seem to be overwhelmed, Christ is in the boat with us.

"Blessed are those who mourn." Blessed are we who struggle with failure, sin, grief, and loss. Blessed, peaceful, with shalom in our hearts are we who mourn, for we shall be comforted. Christ is in the boat with us amid the storms of life. Christ is on the cross with us, whatever our cross may be. Our crosses are never as great as the cross of Christ. Christ is with us in our struggles. We are never alone even when we mourn. We shall be comforted. "Come to me all you who are struggling, fearful, burdened. You shall receive peace."

Let's bring before the Lord now whatever it may be in our hearts—perhaps fear, perhaps a temptation, perhaps a present sorrow, perhaps anxiety, perhaps a failure, maybe a consciousness of limitation—whatever it may be that causes us to mourn. Let's bring it before the Lord and say, "Help me, O Lord. Blessed are those who mourn. Comfort me, O Lord. For they shall be comforted."

> *Blessed are those who mourn, for they shall be comforted.*

༷

> *Blessed are the meek, for they shall inherit the earth.*

This beatitude doesn't make sense according to the way things usually go. Often, people are looking out for number one. Being meek is not usually seen as a formula for success. I can't recall ever going into a bookstore and seeing these titles: *Be Meek: You'll Get Ahead in the World,* or *How to Get a Million Dollars by Being Meek.* It's the opposite. Jesus' words are counterintuitive. We should be meek and gentle—like Moses. Moses was the leader of the people, yet the meekest man around. He was gentle, and he didn't push himself forward. He recognized that all that he did, all that was there, was really from the Lord our God, not from himself. Being

meek involves getting rid of that ego, the desire to domi-
nate, to push down, and to rise up by pushing someone else
down.

Being meek is gentleness, a gentleness that is a freedom,
because only if we are secure in our own heart, do we have
the courage to be meek. Sometimes we feel that we have
to be always pushing, pushing, pushing ahead. If we really
have that trust—that we are to be a feather on the breath of
God—then we have the freedom to be meek, and no need
to show that we are powerful by dominating all the rest.
Blessed are the meek who imitate the One who is meek and
humble of heart for they shall inherit the earth. It really is
that way. Those who do not see this may for a moment push
forward, but what is it worth after all? In order to inherit the
earth, to reach the goal, we need to have a spirit of surrender
in the presence of the Lord, and not to be caught up in the
illusion of our own ego. Being meek doesn't mean not being
strong or not using the gifts God gives us. Absolutely, we
must celebrate our gifts. Yes, but they are gifts, not our own;
they come from the Lord. Therefore we must be meek and
humble of heart in the use of the gifts the Lord gives to us.

"Blessed are the meek, for they shall inherit the earth." Let
us ask the Lord's forgiveness for the times that we have been
so insecure, so truly weak of heart that we have been violent
in word or deed, that we have pushed ourselves forward to
the detriment of others. Pray to the Lord: "Help me, Lord,
to be meek like you, gentle and humble of heart that I may
be a feather on the breath of God, not caught up in my own
ego."

*Blessed are the meek, for they shall inherit the
earth.*

❦

*Blessed are those who hunger and thirst for righ-
teousness, for they shall be satisfied.*

Our Lord has told us to be meek; now he tells us to
hunger and thirst for righteousness. This message from the
Gospel is like a diamond with many facets: each facet reveals
a different aspect of the one message of Christ. One facet
is that we are to be meek like the Lord. Another is that we
are to hunger and thirst for righteousness, for justice in this
world. If we do, we shall be satisfied. This is the fire that
the Lord calls us to have in our hearts. We are even called
to have righteous indignation. If I see evil in this world and
I simply say, "Well, I'll be meek; that's OK; everything is
fine"—that's not the message of the Gospel of Jesus Christ.
He says, "Blessed are the meek." So I shouldn't use my ego
to push someone down. But he also says, "Blessed are those
who hunger and thirst for righteousness, for they shall be
satisfied." Being meek and thirsting for righteousness are
two sides of the Christian life. They are two different aspects
of the same reality. And so meek I must always be, but also
hungering and thirsting for righteousness and justice in this
world. For only then shall I be satisfied.

Let's pray to the Lord to give each one of us that hunger
and thirst for righteousness, so that we do not become complacent. As you might have heard someone say, "The Gospel
is to comfort the afflicted, and to afflict the comfortable."
This is what we have in the beatitudes, these different facets
of the diamond of the message of Christ. Any one of us may
fixate on one or the other of them, but that's not the Gospel. The Gospel is the whole message. The word "Catholic"
means the whole thing, not fixating on one verse or another

verse. Pope Benedict recently called this wholeness the "Catholic *and*." This is what we need to remember. We need to be meek, but we need to hunger and thirst for righteousness, for only then shall we be satisfied. Do we have that fire? Do we show it? Do the actions of our hands show it? Or are we just complacent Christians?

> *Blessed are those who hunger and thirst for righteousness, for they shall be satisfied.*

> ⌒

> *Blessed are the merciful, for they shall obtain mercy.*

In the gospels we often hear parables of mercy. Remember the parable of the one who is forgiven much, and then is demanding of his fellow servants? He was so caught up in his own ego that he did not show mercy to others. The Master does not abide that. "Lord Jesus Christ, Son of God, have mercy on me, a sinner." We ask mercy of the Lord in that profound prayer that we say at every Mass: "Lord, have mercy. Christ, have mercy. Lord, have mercy." As we say it, we need to be conscious of our own sin. We need to stand at the back of the church and say, "Lord, be merciful to me, a sinner."

We also have to remember: "Blessed are the merciful." How often do we become angry because of what we believe is an injustice done to us? We try to defend ourselves: "In fact, it was an injustice and let me prove it to you. I was right and here are fifteen reasons why." And those reasons are correct, aren't they? But what's the point? Let it go. Life is short. We don't have time to waste in proving ourselves right. "Blessed are the merciful." Let it go. "For they shall be shown mercy." How many times have we been shown mercy? That's why the sacrament of reconciliation is so important.

Let's consider confession. You can't get a better opening line than, "Bless me father, for I have sinned." What we might find much more interesting is, "Bless me father, for my neighbor has sinned." No. "Bless me father for *I* have sinned." Let's get out the things that we need to ask mercy for. And if I can dump out the garbage of my heart and recognize that I need God's mercy, maybe it will be a little harder after confession for me to be so demanding on others, even those who might be in the wrong. For are we not also so often wrong? "Blessed are the merciful, for they shall obtain mercy."

Let's ask the Lord to help us to calm down, to lighten up, and not be so demanding of other people. We forget that if anyone held us to the standard to which we hold other people, we wouldn't survive for a moment. That's why we need to get to confession. We need to do that a lot. It helps us. At the end of the day, it's also a great idea to look over our day using whatever checklist we want, (I use the seven deadly sins—pride, anger, envy, greed, laziness, lust, gluttony—or the Ten Commandments) and say, "Lord Jesus Christ, Son of God, have mercy on me, a sinner." And then quietly throughout the day—no one need ever know—just pray the beautiful Jesus Prayer: "Lord Jesus Christ, Son of God, have mercy on me, a sinner." Through the entire day, pray the Jesus Prayer. Or sometimes pray the rosary, using the Jesus Prayer instead of the Hail Mary. "Blessed are the merciful, for they shall obtain mercy." Let's pray, "Lord, help me to be more merciful to other people, to be less critical, to be less censorious, noting every little speck." Let us say, "Lord Jesus Christ, Son of God, have mercy on *me*, a sinner."

Blessed are the merciful, for they shall obtain mercy.

～

Blessed are the pure in heart, for they shall see God.

None of us can say, "I'm pure in heart." We're all caught up in so much that's not quite pure; that's why we need to ask the Lord for his mercy. We need to say: "Lord, help me to be pure of heart. Let me be crystal clear all the way through." So often I need to ask for the Lord's mercy because I am like glass that has lots of bubbles in it, so twisted and turned that the light of Christ won't shine through.

I remember once going to a glass museum in Corning, New York. There were two fairly long pieces of glass (4–5 feet long) with a well-lit picture at the end of each one. When I looked into the piece made of ordinary glass, I could barely see a smudge at the bottom. When I looked down the other, I could see clearly to the end. One piece was ordinary glass with bubbles of air and twists, and the other was pure crystal all the way through. Let me be the pure and clear crystal.

Let's not play games—pretending to be nice to other people, but really following our own agenda. Blessed are the pure of heart. Let's not play games. Let's be pure. Say, "Lord help me." Purity of heart is to will one thing. God is simple. We get complicated. The more we are like God, the more we will be simple and upfront, and pure of heart: what you see is what you get. "Oh what a tangled web we weave, when first we practice to deceive." Too often, we're trying to keep several layers going at once. And for what purpose? Why do we make life so complicated? Life is too short to be complicated. Let's be who we are and say, "Lord, help me to be pure of heart."

Ask for the Lord's forgiveness in our own hearts for the times we put a lot of lead into the pure gold we received from the Lord. And say, "Away with that. Jesus, Jesus, come to me. From all my sins, set me free. Help me to be pure of heart so I shall see God." When we are all twisted inside, God's light can't get through, and we ourselves can't see. We need to be pure of heart in order to see clearly. When we're not pure of heart, it's like we're driving down the highway with a blanket over the windshield: comfortable for a moment, but not fundamentally safe. Help me, O Lord, to be pure in heart.

> *Blessed are the pure in heart, for they shall see God.*

✎

> *Blessed are the peacemakers, for they shall be called sons of God.*

There is so much conflict in this world with war and violence, so much within our own private world, so much within our own hearts. If the individual heart has no peace, there will be no peace within the world. So we need to be peacemakers. Working for peace doesn't mean we need to be meddling in things. We need to say: "Lord, how can I bring peace in this situation I'm dealing with in my life? How can I help bring peace in the wider world?" Peace is not simply an absence of violence, but peace is that serenity, that harmony, that music of God, which reflects the very life of the inner Trinity, that inner life of generous love of the Father, Son, and Holy Spirit. We're made in the image and likeness of the Blessed Trinity. We're made to live in the name of the Father,

Son, and Holy Spirit in love and peace with one another and with peace in our own hearts. "Blessed are the peacemakers." We can be peacemakers even (or perhaps most profoundly) by praying for peace. Begin by contributing to this world love and forgiveness first. Then, if we can think of something we could do practically in this or that situation that will bring peace, let us do it and not just sit on the sideline. Let us do it rightly and wisely. We can begin to make this happen by asking the Lord for the gift of wisdom.

> *Blessed are the peacemakers, for they shall be called sons of God.*

Blessed are those who are persecuted for righ-teousness' sake, for theirs is the kingdom of heaven. Blessed are you when men revile you and persecute you and utter all kinds of evil against you falsely on my account. Rejoice and be glad, for your reward is great in heaven, for so men persecuted the prophets who were before you.

"Blessed are those who are persecuted for righteousness' sake, for theirs is the kingdom of heaven." If we are faithful to the Lord, then it is likely that we are going to experience resistance. St. Thomas More once said that we don't get "to go to heaven on feather beds." In this world, there are so many people being persecuted. Many of our brothers and sisters in Christ today are in danger of death—even more so now than in the Roman Empire during the first centuries. Let us pray for them. Let us reach out and do something to help.

"Blessed are those who are persecuted for righteousness' sake." Let's not ever be a persecutor, because as we know, we *can* persecute. We get caught up with self-righteousness, with a glint in the eye and fire in the heart. How often have people in the name of the Lord struck out at others: "You will believe, or else." Such threats are not the way of Christ.

"Blessed are those who are persecuted for righteousness' sake, for theirs is the kingdom of heaven. Blessed are you when men revile you and persecute you and utter all kinds of evil against you falsely on my account. Rejoice and be glad, for your reward is great in heaven, for so men persecuted the prophets who were before you." Would anyone take any of us seriously enough to persecute us? That is a question to think about. "Blessed are you when men revile you and persecute you and utter all kinds of evil against you falsely on my account." I think: "If I go along and get along, no one will ever utter anything against me. I'll just slide through life." But, have I ever done anything worthwhile enough to get me persecuted? If I were arrested for being a Christian, would there be enough evidence to convict me?

"Blessed are *you*." In each of the preceding beatitudes, Jesus has said, "Blessed are *they*." Now he says, "Blessed are *you*." Our Lord ends with a bang. "Blessed are *you* when men revile you and persecute you and utter all kinds of evil against you falsely on my account." And look what he says here in the midst of all these challenges: "Rejoice and be glad, for your reward is great in heaven, for so men persecuted the prophets who were before you."

I often think of the great St. Thomas More in his final letters, his last words before he gave his life for Christ. He was fond of saying—even to the people betraying him—"Let us meet merrily in Heaven." He was about to be beheaded, yet he cracked jokes all the way up to the scaffold. He said to the executioner, "Help me on the way up. I'll take care of myself on the way down." As he put his head on the block, he said, "Be sure you aim right so that you don't ruin your reputation." St. Thomas More was being persecuted for his righteousness; he was pure of heart, trusting, poor in spirit. He's a model for the way we all should be.

∽

Please reread the scripture passage at the beginning of the chapter (pages 1–2).

∽

Our Father

Hail Mary

Glory Be

Chapter Two

Matthew 5:13–26

Speak, Lord; your servant is listening.

Come Holy Spirit, fill the hearts of your faithful, and enkindle in us the fire of your love. Send forth your Spirit, and we shall be created, and you shall renew the face of the earth.

Speak, Lord; your servant is listening.

You are the salt of the earth; but if salt has lost its taste, how shall its saltness be restored? It is no longer good for anything except to be thrown out and trodden under foot by men. You are the light of the world. A city set on a hill cannot be hid. Nor do men light a lamp and put it under a bushel, but on a stand, and it gives light to all in the house. Let your light so shine before men, that they may see your good works and give glory to your Father who is in heaven. Think not that I have come to abolish the law and the prophets; I have come not to abolish them but to fulfil them. For truly, I say to you, till heaven and earth pass away, not an iota, not a dot, will pass from the law until all is accomplished. Whoever then relaxes one of the least of these commandments and teaches men so, shall be called least in the kingdom of heaven; but he who does them and teaches them shall be called great in the kingdom of heaven. For I tell you, unless your righteousness exceeds that of the scribes and Pharisees, you will never enter the kingdom of heaven. You have heard that it was said to the men of old, "You shall not kill; and whoever kills shall be liable to judgment." But I say to you that every one who is angry with his brother shall be liable to judgment; whoever insults his brother shall be liable to the council, and whoever says, "You fool!" shall be liable to the hell of fire. So if you are offering your gift at the altar, and there remember that your brother has something against you, leave your gift there before the altar and go; first be reconciled to your brother, and then come and offer your gift. Make friends quickly with your accuser, while you are going with him to court, lest your accuser hand you over to the judge, and the judge to the guard, and you be put in prison; truly, I say to you, you will never get out till you have paid the last penny.

Spend a moment now reflecting upon this section of the Sermon on the Mount. What is one point that our Lord makes that applies most fully to my life?

❧

You are the salt of the earth; but if salt has lost its taste, how shall its saltness be restored? It is no longer good for anything except to be thrown out and trodden under foot by men.

We are the salt of the earth. We are to be that lively force that adds zest to this world. Our Lord says to us that we are "the salt of the earth." Salt purifies; it adds spice to life. It would be terrible if as Christians we were rather bland. We can't be content to just go along with our own lives, with little effort to make a difference. We are called to be "the salt of the earth."

In this world which so often is filled with corruption and evil, we are to be that salt that helps purify it and make it strong and true, conserves it and gives it zest. Some writers have described evil as being banal and bland. They are right. The evil of this world is really not all that exciting; it is dull and flat, lacking in hope. The great poet Dante wrote in his *Inferno* that over the gateway of hell are written the words: "Abandon hope, all you who enter here." The pathway of evil is without salt, without zest, without hope. That pathway is not for us in the short journey of life.

Our Lord calls us to get off the pathway to evil. He calls us to be more and do more. He says, "You are the salt of the earth." We have to be more. We have to be that salt that gives this whole world its zest, its fire, its excitement, and that joy that comes from the Christian life.

Our Lord also warns that the salt can start losing its taste and power, especially if it's diluted and mixed in with other things. We're called to be the salt of the earth, and yet how flat can that salt be! It can be left to go flat, without taste and zest, unless we look after it. We do not attract people to Christ if we are simply living in a bland way, blending with the world that surrounds us. We're meant to be different; we're meant to be the salt that brings spice to the world. We're meant to bring the fire of the presence of the Lord to our world. Sometimes, it seems that we cannot live up to that goal. The salt in our own lives has gone flat. Without this salt at work in our own lives, we cannot really bring that experience of the flavor of the Lord to other people.

So let's just listen to these words now, and ask the question: In my own life, to what degree am I contributing something to the world around me? Am I bringing to my world the spice and the zest that salt brings to food? Is my own ability to spice up the world with the zest of the Gospel weakened because I don't have very much salt myself? If I've gone flat, then I can hardly provide seasoning. You know the old saying: "We can't give what we haven't got."

Here is a little examination of conscience on what the Lord says to us about being salt of the earth. Not only does he say, "Your mission, should you choose to accept it, is to be salt of the earth," but also he tells us if we lack that spice ourselves, if we are just flat, then we cannot share that zest with others. So we need to look within our hearts, and listen to these words, and say, "Lord help me to be filled with that salt, with that spice of the Gospel, so that I can share the gift with others whom I meet each day."

Let's spend a little time now reflecting on his words and encountering the Lord and saying, "Lord Jesus, what are you saying to me in my life as I hear these words?"

> *You are the salt of the earth; but if salt has lost*
> *its taste, how shall its saltness be restored? It is no*

*longer good for anything except to be thrown out
and trodden under foot by men.*

❧

*You are the light of the world. A city set on a hill
cannot be hid. Nor do men light a lamp and put
it under a bushel, but on a stand, and it gives
light to all in the house. Let your light so shine
before men, that they may see your good works
and give glory to your Father who is in heaven.*

"You are the light of the world." Christ is the light of the
world, and he says to us, "*You* are the light of the world." At
the Easter Vigil, and in the Evening Prayer ceremony of the
light, we see the light of Christ carried into the darkened
church. Then we reach out with our little candles to catch
that fire, and then to share it with our neighbor until the
whole church is bright with the light of Christ. We receive
that fire from the Lord. He says, "You are the light of the
world," but first we've got to take our little candle and reach
out to the light of Christ. We are the light of the world, if we
receive it from Christ.

Every day we need to be in touch with the fire; we need
to reach out to see and find it and keep it bright within our
own hearts so that we can share it with others. He says, "You
are the light of the world." We need to reflect upon that and
say, "Lord, help me to be the light to others you call me
to be. And help me to find that light by the reading of the
sacred scriptures, by taking time for prayer every day." When
our Lord invited the apostles he said, "Come and see." We
come to him to experience who he is. If we are with him,
then we can receive that fire. And then we can be the light

of the world—not just our own little light, flashing around ineffectually. "You are the light of the world." Lord, help me to be a light to other people.

How am I called in my own mission in life, in my own work, to most effectively be the light of Christ to the world? What is one practical way, today, that I can be a light to the people around me?

"You are the light of the world." It's hard to share the light if we blow it out. It's not enough just to receive it from Christ. If we receive light from Christ and then blow it out, we can't give it to other people. So if I'm to be the light of the world—and that's what my mission is—then I need to ask, "What are the ways in which I blow out or darken the light of Christ?" Pride, anger, envy, greed, laziness, lust, and gluttony are things that darken the light of Christ, that extinguish the light of Christ within my heart. So if I am to be the light of the world—the mission received in baptism and confirmation—then I need to lead a repentant life. This is the reason we begin every Mass with, "Lord, have mercy." As we come before the Lord himself to receive the fire of the Blessed Sacrament, we recognize that within our own hearts there are places that are very dark and that need to be purified. "Lord, have mercy. Christ, have mercy. Lord, have mercy." So we need to lead a repentant life, to let the light shine, and not blow it out by our own selfishness and sin.

What are the ways today in which we have blown out the light of Christ within us, so that we cannot share it with others? Let's think of one action, one thought, one experience today where we have blown out the light of Christ. Let's ask the Lord's forgiveness for those times of darkness. Say, "Lord have mercy, Christ have mercy, Lord have mercy. Help me to be more light-giving tomorrow."

You are the light of the world. A city set on a hill cannot be hid. Nor do men light a lamp and put it under a bushel, but on a stand, and it gives light to all in the house. Let your light so shine before men, that they may see your good works and give glory to your Father who is in heaven.

⌒

You are the light of the world. A city set on a hill cannot be hid. Nor do men light a lamp and put it under a bushel, but on a stand, and it gives light to all in the house. Let your light so shine before men, that they may see your good works and give glory to your Father who is in heaven.

We're not called to be timid if we're Christians. We're meant to shed that light . . . to let our light shine. "A city set on a hill cannot be hid." We're meant to move forward, not aggressively, but assertively within this world, letting the light of Christ shine. And we do that sometimes by what we say, sometimes by what we do, but most of all by who we are. We have received that light within us, and we ask God's forgiveness for the times when we extinguish it through our selfishness. I can't cling to the light for myself, because it's meant to be given to others. "A city set on a hill cannot be hid. Nor do men light a lamp and put it under a bushel, but on a stand, and it gives light to all in the house. Let your light so shine before men that they may see your good works and give glory to your Father who is in heaven."

We're not supposed to do good works while saying, "Look at me; I've done good things." Our Lord says in the Sermon on the Mount, "Your Father in heaven sees." We don't need to be flaunting our good works in an egotistical way. But we *are* meant to be the salt of the earth, the light of the world. And so, individually and as a Church, we're meant to shine brightly and to engage in this world. Where there is darkness, let us bring the light of Christ. We are not to be timid, hiding the light of Christ.

In his writings, St. Paul declares the need for boldness. Think of how St. Paul launched into Europe and brought the light of Christ. He didn't hold back. Nor did he get worried when the darkness began to swirl around him. So often we can become too timid when darkness happens. We can, in very cowardly ways, avoid shedding the light of Christ as we are called to do. What's the point of putting the light of the Gospel under a bushel basket and hiding it? It's meant to be on a stand.

We need to be humble, never flaunting our good works as if they're our own. But we are called to let Christ's light shine brightly in this world, and—as individual Christians, as parishes and dioceses, as the whole universal Church—to have that spirit of joyful boldness through which we let the light of Christ shine. We can see this adventurous spirit of the Christian life in the first disciples. We see it in the Acts of the Apostles, when the apostles burst out of the upper room at Pentecost. Remember the signs of Pentecost—the wind that blows and the fire that comes down upon the apostles? What we're called to be, this light of Christ, is Pentecostal fire. We show it, not through grand, extravagant experiences, but by the way in which in our thoughts, our words, our actions, we radiate the light of Christ into this world.

Let's reflect upon the light and say, "Lord, help me in my life not to be timid and hesitant about my faith. Not to dip my toe into the pool of life, but to dive in. Let that light shine in me. Help me, oh Lord, to let your light shine brightly and to bring that light where it is most in need."

You are the light of the world. A city set on a hill cannot be hid. Nor do men light a lamp and put it under a bushel, but on a stand, and it gives light to all in the house. Let your light so shine before men, that they may see your good works and give glory to your Father who is in heaven.

Think not that I have come to abolish the law and the prophets; I have come not to abolish them but to fulfil them. For truly, I say to you, till heaven and earth pass away, not an iota, not a dot, will pass from the law until all is accomplished. Whoever then relaxes one of the least of these commandments and teaches men so, shall be called least in the kingdom of heaven; but he who does them and teaches them shall be called great in the kingdom of heaven. For I tell you, unless your righteousness exceeds that of the scribes and Pharisees, you will never enter the kingdom of heaven.

In the law and the prophets of the Old Testament, we find the word of God. It is unfinished, reaching out for fulfillment. Every Sunday at Mass we have the first reading, which is from the Old Testament. The first reading is always chosen in light of the gospel of the day—which brings it to fulfillment. Life and light are found within the Old Testament, reaching outward to the completion in Christ.

One of the first heresies of the Christian Church was created by a man called Marcion, who wanted to eliminate the Old Testament and to use just the New Testament. He even wanted to remove from the New Testament those things that

were from the Old Testament, which would lead to a New
Testament about the size of a scrap of paper. And the Church
said, "No, no; that's not the way. The Lord's revelation is one
piece; it is a seamless garment." The New Testament fulfills
the Old Testament, but it doesn't replace it.

Later in the Sermon on the Mount, our Lord says, "You
have heard this, but I say to you . . ." The way the Lord speaks
might be misunderstood as meaning that Christ is replacing
the Old Testament. Christ didn't come to make the law and
the prophets obsolete, but to fulfill them. The richness of the
law and the prophets in the Old Testament still gives life, but
it needs to be brought to completion. And Christ addresses
this problem, saying at the end of the passage that he takes
the old law very seriously: "For I tell you, unless your righteousness exceeds that of the scribes and Pharisees you will
never enter the kingdom of heaven."

The kingdom of heaven is the great promise of the Lord
to us. Christ emphasizes that our righteousness has to be
greater than that demonstrated by the scribes and Pharisees.
Righteousness involves living according to the words of the
Sermon on the Mount, being salt and light in this world.
Our righteousness must not be narrow or harsh or centered
on our own working out of salvation, but should be the joyful boldness of a disciple of the Lord. And it is rooted in the
Gospel, whose foundation is the Law and the prophets of
the Old Testament. The Bible is one great gift of the Lord;
we need to be immersed in the whole of the sacred scripture,
watching its fulfillment in the Gospel.

Sometimes, as we read the parts of the Law of the Lord
that lead up to Christ, we feel them speak to us very power-
fully. The Ten Commandments speak to us always. They're
still in force. They're not the ten suggestions; they're the Ten
Commandments. And they're still there to lead us to the

Lord. We can't get caught up in the view that the God of
the Old Testament is the God of wrath, while the God of the
New Testament is the God of love; no . . . God is God.
The God of love who says that you shall love the Lord your
God with heart and mind and soul, and that you shall love
your neighbor as yourself, is quoting the Old Testament passages from Deuteronomy and Leviticus. The New Testament
is fulfilling the Old Testament. There is no division.

We shouldn't think that the God of the New Testament is
some kind of special different Lord, who simply says, "That's
okay, do whatever you want; I was a little more strict in the
Old Testament, but now let's just love, love, love . . . don't
worry. Have a nice day." I think not. In fact, later on in Matthew's gospel, Matthew reminds us that our choices have
consequences. We hear of the sheep and the goats: remember
the story of the separation of the sheep from the goats on the
last day? Life ends with judgment.

Our Lord is the Lord of love, the Lord of life, the Lord of
justice, and the Lord of mercy and compassion. But his truth
is all one piece, one seamless garment. We need to live it to
the full. We can't be solely Old Testament people or New
Testament people, as if those were contradictory. So let's listen to the words of the Lord, and then as we hear them, say,
"Lord, help me in my own life to be immersed in the words
of sacred scripture. Help me be immersed in the law of the
Lord that is found in the Old Testament, which is sweeter
than honey from the honeycomb. Help me be immersed in
that great fulfillment of the Old Testament which is found in
our Lord Jesus Christ, and in the words of the Holy Gospel,
where it's all one piece, one gift of God."

> *Think not that I have come to abolish the law
> and the prophets; I have come not to abolish*

them but to fulfil them. For truly, I say to you, till heaven and earth pass away, not an iota, not a dot, will pass from the law until all is accomplished. Whoever then relaxes one of the least of these commandments and teaches men so, shall be called least in the kingdom of heaven; but he who does them and teaches them shall be called great in the kingdom of heaven. For I tell you, unless your righteousness exceeds that of the scribes and Pharisees, you will never enter the kingdom of heaven.

Our Lord now begins to speak of six ways in which he fulfills the law of God. He calls us to greatness, calls us to a depth of life that allows each one of us to be salt of the earth and light to the world. Now we will pray the first section on those ways in which he fulfills the Old Testament laws, and in the following chapter we will pray the others.

You have heard that it was said to the men of old, "You shall not kill; and whoever kills shall be liable to judgment." But I say to you that every one who is angry with his brother shall be liable to judgment; whoever insults his brother shall be liable to the council, and whoever says, "You fool!" shall be liable to the hell of fire.

"Thou shalt not kill." This is the word of God, which Moses, the great Moses brought down from Mt. Sinai: "Thou shalt not kill." Jesus repeats this message for all to hear because it is an important message. "You have heard . . . , but I say to you . . ." In this passage, not only do we hear the content of the lesson on murder, we encounter the voice of God teaching us directly: "But *I* say to you." No one can speak in that way of the great law of the Lord who is not the Lord God himself amongst us.

Elsewhere in the gospels, when we hear "I am," it is the Lord speaking. As Christians we have teachings that we've received from the Lord. The Sermon on the Mount is a kind of a summary of his teachings, as in a sense the Beatitudes are a summary of the Sermon on the Mount. This is the teaching of the Master, which makes us light and salt for the world. It comes from the lips of the Master who is God-with-us, our Lord and Savior, Jesus Christ. So as we hear these words, we notice their incredible personal call to us: ". . . but I say to *you*." He calls out to us.

"But I say to you that everyone who is angry with his brother shall be liable to judgment; whoever insults his brother shall be liable to the council, and whoever says 'You fool!' shall be liable to the hell of fire."

It's not enough just simply to say, "Thou shalt not kill." What leads to the killing is the anger that grows inside. What we do comes from internal sources. Remember that elsewhere in the gospel Jesus speaks about how all kinds of foulness come from within, from the heart. Certainly we are to avoid the sins such as killing—the acts themselves. But more than that: we must be crystal clear all the way through. We need to be purified, not letting anger fester within us.

Of course, the emotion of anger is something that we feel just naturally; it's a natural response. If somebody steps on my foot, I will have a reaction to that. If somebody does something cruel, I'll have a reaction. That's normal. It's not a sin; it's our human response. But perhaps then I begin to stew in the acid of that anger, and it begins to eat away at me. My mind begins to race around and around with the injustice of it all. I start thinking with hatred toward that person. Long before I might go to the extreme of killing, my life is being absorbed by the force of darkness, and I cannot be the light of Christ in this world.

Our Lord says to us, "But I say to you that everyone who is angry with his brother shall be liable to judgment; whoever insults his brother shall be liable to the council, and whoever says, 'You fool!' shall be liable to the hell of fire." What disdain we have within us, so often thinking, "You fool, you fool." How easily we dismiss people. In our consumer culture, we are very accustomed to throwing out the trash. We throw people away in that way too, with our words and our thoughts: "You fool. You're not worth a moment of my time." We let our disdain take root in our heart long before we get to the stage of taking physical action. So our Lord calls us to think deeply, to look deeply within our hearts. He reminds us that it's not enough just to say, "I have not killed." We've got to go deeper, to look at the anger that can so consume us. We've got to say, "Lord forgive me," and let it go. If I'm stewing within, I am not resolving whatever it is that caused the anger; I am just darkening the light of Christ; and so I can't be salt of the earth and light to the world. ·

You know that when we make an act of contrition, we say, "Let me avoid the near occasions of sin"? To be able to handle sin is so important. We might say, "Don't worry, I'm not going to the extreme." Perhaps not, but we need to address the causes of our emotions. We need to handle our anger, but also our pride, envy, greed, laziness, lust, and gluttony, too. We've got to think not just of the ultimate acts of sinning, but we need to address the roots as well. Then we can be the light of this world and the salt of this earth.

Let's reflect again upon this as our Lord speaks to us:

You have heard that it was said to the men of old, "You shall not kill; and whoever kills shall be liable to judgment." But I say to you that every one who is angry with his brother shall be liable to judgment; whoever insults his brother shall be liable to the council, and whoever says, "You fool!" shall be liable to the hell of fire.

Let's ask the Lord's forgiveness for the times in our life when we have been absorbed in a fruitless anger toward other people.

⌁

So if you are offering your gift at the altar, and there remember that your brother has something against you, leave your gift there before the altar and go; first be reconciled to your brother, and then come and offer your gift. Make friends quickly with your accuser, while you are going with him to court, lest your accuser hand you over to the judge, and the judge to the guard, and you be put in prison; truly, I say to you, you will never get out till you have paid the last penny.

Our Lord uses a couple of strategies here. First he tells us to be at peace with our brother. Then he says, be at peace or we're going to get thrown in jail. He knows we need various incentives to help us to understand what's important. What he's describing is really what we do at Mass while offering the sign of peace, when we say, "Peace be with you." When we offer our gifts at the altar, we say, "Peace be with you." Before we receive our blessed Lord himself, we say, "Peace be with you." We don't say, "Hi, have a nice day." We don't offer a vapid hello. We offer the peace of Christ. And if somewhere in the church there's someone who has made me angry, or who has done something that has hurt me, or if I have wronged someone, then I start climbing over the pews to say, "Peace be with *you*." Now, that might be more than is necessary, like going to confession in public. It's sufficient and symbolic enough to turn and say to whoever is nearby, "Peace be with you; peace be with you."

I remember going to a monastery once—there they offer the sign of peace in the formal way where you put your arms on the shoulders of the monk next to you and solemnly move your head in a symbolic kiss of peace to one side and then the other. I'm not very well coordinated; I was bumping heads with the monk very awkwardly. Probably a simpler way is the shaking of hands or saying, "Peace be with you," while making a simple bow in the direction of the person nearby.

Understandably, we often happen to be near our friends or our family during the sign of peace. Within the circle of our friends and our family we might have hurt someone, or someone might have hurt us. But giving the sign of peace isn't restricted to the people we like. If anything, giving the sign of peace is more like—at least figuratively speaking—hopping over the pews to get to the person you've hurt or who has hurt you. Giving the sign of peace could be a very sublime experience of what our Lord is talking about in this verse. We turn to the person, and we could be thinking, "I can't stand you. Your personality rubs me the wrong way. Your political views are outrageous. Your taste in clothes is abominable. I would not want to go on a trip with you." But then we say aloud: "The peace of Christ be with you." That's the heart of it all.

Now I do not recommend putting into voice those thoughts we might harbor about those around us. This could lead to fistfights throughout the church—which might tend to defeat the purpose. But this reaching out to those with whom we do not get along is what our Lord is talking about here. This deep peace, this shalom of Christ, goes beyond all those other petty annoyances and helps us to see our brother and sister in Christ so we can say, "Forgive me for the times I have sinned, and I forgive you." We cannot forgive and forget, because rarely can we completely forget. We are not expected to do the impossible; but we are called upon to forgive. Forgiving means to be at peace with the other person and not to be stewing in the anger that robs life of its salt and light, making us shrivel up. We don't have time for that. We're meant to be salt and light to the world.

∽

Please reread the scripture passage at the beginning of the chapter (pages 17–18).

∽

Our Father

Hail Mary

Glory Be

CHAPTER THREE

Matthew 5:27–37

Speak, Lord; your servant is listening.

Come, Holy Spirit, fill the hearts of your faithful, and enkindle in us the fire of your love. Send forth your Spirit, and we shall be created, and you shall renew the face of the earth.

Let's let go of all those distractions, the worries that concern us, all of the inner struggles that so distract us and fill our hearts and minds, leaving no room for the word of the Lord. Away with all those things; just let them go.

Speak, Lord; your servant is listening.

You have heard that it was said, "You shall not commit adultery." But I say to you that every one who looks at a woman lustfully has already committed adultery with her in his heart. If your right eye causes you to sin, pluck it out and throw it away; it is better that you lose one of your members than that your whole body be thrown into hell. And if your right hand causes you to sin, cut it off and throw it away; it is better that you lose one of your members than that your whole body go into hell. It was also said, "Who-ever divorces his wife, let him give her a certifi-cate of divorce." But I say to you that every one who divorces his wife, except on the ground of unchastity, makes her an adulteress; and whoever marries a divorced woman commits adultery. Again you have heard that it was said to the men of old, "You shall not swear falsely, but shall perform to the Lord what you have sworn." But I say to you, Do not swear at all, either by heaven, for it is the throne of God, or by the earth, for it is his footstool, or by Jerusalem, for it is the city of the great King. And do not swear by your head, for you cannot make one hair white or black. Let what you say be simply "Yes" or "No"; anything more than this comes from evil.

～

You have heard that it was said, "You shall not commit adultery." But I say to you that every one who looks at a woman lustfully has already com-mitted adultery with her in his heart.

Just before mentioning adultery, our Lord was speaking about anger and killing. He said that not only should we avoid the action, but that we should address the root cause of killing, which is anger. In this passage, he reflects upon another one of the seven deadly sins—lust. Pride, anger, envy, greed, laziness, lust, and gluttony are the seven roots of sin. Each one of them is a source of struggle, and some people struggle more with one or another. A very good form of examination of conscience is to go down that list, and to reflect upon the ways in which these roots of darkness might have a grip upon our hearts.

"You have heard that it was said, 'You shall not commit adultery.' But I say to you that everyone who looks at a woman lustfully has already committed adultery with her in his heart." I think this is an equal-opportunity verse, applying equally to both men and women. Shakespeare has something to say on the topic as well. He tells us that "The expense of spirit in a waste of shame is lust in action" (Sonnet 129). There's a saying that we're freed from the temptation to lust ten minutes after we're dead. I don't know whether that's technically true or not, but lust certainly is a strong force in many lives. As our Lord says, it is simply not enough to avoid committing adultery; the Lord speaks here of the way that every sinful action, whether it be lust or whether it be one of the other deadly sins, has its root within the heart. Elsewhere he says that out of the heart evil can come.

And so the Lord makes his point clear. He speaks to us as our Lord, who is giving us a new vision: "I say to you that everyone who looks at a woman lustfully has already committed adultery with her in his heart."

Whether it be lust or whether it be any of the other deadly sins that trouble us, we need to deal with the root of the sin, looking to our heart, at our intentions. If we deal with the root causes, then we're not so likely to get into the external manifestations of sin. I remember a story of General MacArthur. I think he was retreating to Australia during the Second World War. He heard someone say, "We will fight the enemy in the very streets of our capital." And he replied, "No, I'd rather fight the enemy a thousand miles away, long before it gets to that point." This is why we pray to avoid the near occasions of sin, and why we need to watch for venial sins. Those little things that are, in themselves perhaps not so great, can lead us on to other things.

I think our Lord asks us to use good common sense; don't put gasoline all over the floor and start lighting matches, or you're going to cause something to happen. And we can't just simply deal with a problem when it has reached its final stage. So, for a bit of strategy that all of us need for handling sin in our lives, one of the wise things to do is to look to the near occasions of sin, to the things that lead us in the direction of darkness. We know from our own past history that "someone else might be able to handle this situation, but I cannot." We need to identify within our own hearts, within the geography of our soul, those things that may lead us astray.

One reason for looking at the intentions of the heart is to prevent sin from going further, to nip it in the bud. But, of course, our Lord says as well, "I say to you that everyone who looks at a woman lustfully has already committed adultery with her in his heart." It is not just that we need to look to the roots of sin to prevent us from going further. When we are absorbed with our own desires, when we are imploding into ourselves, we leave no room for the Lord. So, we are already sinning through the intention of our heart.

Let's just think for a moment now and pray to the Lord, and say, "Lord, free me from those things within me that I dwell upon, that I draw myself to, that I get absorbed in—things which lead me to deeper forms of darkness and which leave no room for you in my heart." What are they in my own life? They could be lust, greed, anger, or any of the other deadly sins. If they are in my heart, they will become actions as well. Even in the heart they are too much. We need to be free of those things that take us away from the Lord. We need to be free, and we cannot be if these things dwell within our hearts.

So let's ask the Lord's forgiveness for these desires—whatever they might be. Within our own hearts, name what those things are, whether lust, anger, envy, or the other sins. They are darkness within the heart for which we need to ask the Lord's forgiveness.

> *You have heard that it was said, "You shall not commit adultery." But I say to you that every one who looks at a woman lustfully has already committed adultery with her in his heart.*

> *If your right eye causes you to sin, pluck it out and throw it away; it is better that you lose one of your members than that your whole body be thrown into hell. And if your right hand causes you to sin, cut it off and throw it away; it is better that you lose one of your members than that your whole body go into hell.*

This is hyperbole, strong language that the Lord uses to shake us up. As a preacher, he is trying to get through to us and to give that message that makes us listen and reflect. I don't think our Lord is requiring that we all start cutting out eyes and hands, but the point is very clear. He does not want us to harm ourselves, but rather to look inward: our Lord has just said that it is in the heart where sin resides. It is not the eye that sins, but the deeper reality that causes us to sin. He speaks to us forcefully. "If your eye causes you to sin, pluck it out . . . If your hand causes you to sin, cut it off." He's saying that sin is not trivial, that we need to take clear action. We can often drift along, comfortable with our sins, and semi-repenting, but never really taking seriously the call to repentance.

In the Gospel of Matthew, John the Baptist begins his message by saying, "Repent, for the kingdom of heaven is near at hand." We always think of Jesus as kind and gentle, and John the Baptist as a severe, rather scrawny and stern prophet of doom; but remember the first words our Lord Jesus preaches in the same gospel: "Repent, for the kingdom of heaven is near at hand." They are exactly the same as John the Baptist's words.

And so Jesus says, "If your right eye causes you to sin, pluck it out and throw it away." In other words, half measures are not enough. Really get to the root. Take seriously this leaving the way of darkness and coming to the way of light. He uses extreme language, not to tell us to mutilate ourselves, but to tell us to take temptations to sin very seriously. He shakes us up and says, "Listen, sin is not simply something that we weave into the pattern of our lives, something we can live with. It is something that makes us less than we are." When we celebrate the feast of the Immaculate Conception, we reflect upon the fact that from the first moment of her existence, Our Lady was totally in harmony with the will of God. And sometimes we think, "Well, that must mean that she's extraordinary; she's beyond the human." But all it means is—she's just normal. The default setting of the human race should be total harmony with the will of God. When we sin, we're less than what we're meant to be.

And so we make an examination of conscience—be it with the Ten Commandments or the seven deadly sins or some other way—to see all those things within us that are not of the Lord, those things that load us down and with which we have become too comfortable. Those are things we need to rip out and get rid of. "If your eye causes you to sin, pluck it out." This is the seriousness with which we take the spiritual life. And we know that because of our frailty, we face a lifelong struggle. It is a struggle to say every day, "Jesus, Jesus, come to me. From all my sins, oh, set me free. Lord Jesus Christ, Son of God, have mercy on me, a sinner." Every day we can say, "Lord, take away those things within me that turn me away from you."

The Lord does allow us to struggle with our temptations, so that we might grow in humility. It's a lot harder to criticize another person after we've said, "Bless me, father, for I have sinned." We know that even plucking out our eye and cutting off our hand would not rid us of those things for which we need to ask the Lord's forgiveness. We need to be more forgiving to the people around us, whose sins we can see so much easier than our own.

Our Lord is saying to us here: take sin seriously. A life, a normal life, a human life as it is meant to be lived, is a life in harmony with the will of God. And when we're not in harmony, we're not living up to that invitation to deep inner peace and joy which the Lord offers to us. He's with us in the struggle day by day, as we try to resist temptation and to be faithful to the will of our heavenly Father. Pray, "Lord, take from me those things that lead me to sin, and help me to be at peace, to be a person who does your will." At the heart of the Lord's Prayer, we pray, "Thy kingdom come, thy will be done." In this short life of ours, we don't have time for all those things that take us away from the Lord, and yet so often we simply fill our hearts with them. There's no room for the Lord in the inn of our hearts, because we fill them up with so much junk, so many useless things. The Lord calls us to a kind of spring-cleaning here.

It's not easy, because our hearts so often are cold and hard. And yet if we're earnestly saying, "Lord, help me," and "Lord Jesus Christ, son of God, have mercy on me, a sinner," he's always there to lift us up. That's why we go to the sacrament of reconciliation again and again and again. Because, after all, we're frail; and we need to be purified again and again and again.

As we listen to these serious words, let's reflect. As we hear the words of our Lord, which he says in a dramatic way to get our attention, let's look at those things within our life that lead us to sin. Say, "Lord, help me to be freed of these things that leave no room for you."

> *If your right eye causes you to sin, pluck it out and throw it away; it is better that you lose one of your members than that your whole body be thrown into hell. And if your right hand causes you to sin, cut it off and throw it away; it is better that you lose one of your members than that your whole body go into hell.*

ᕓ

> *It was also said, "Whoever divorces his wife, let him give her a certificate of divorce." But I say to you that every one who divorces his wife, except on the ground of unchastity, makes her an adulteress; and whoever marries a divorced woman commits adultery.*

Our Lord speaks here of faithfulness in marriage. Later in the Gospel of St. Matthew, he speaks at length of marriage and celibacy. As we hear this portion of the Sermon on the Mount, it is important to reflect upon the teaching of the Lord elsewhere within this gospel and within all of the gospels. We should reflect and pray and come to understand more his teaching about the meaning of marriage and about the whole meaning of life.

Our Lord here is emphasizing the sacredness of marriage at a time when in his own society, very much like our own, there were words spoken against the covenant of marriage. Our Lord is proclaiming marriage to be that sacred, binding covenant of love between a man and a woman, faithful in love and open to the gift of life. This profound teaching of the Lord, found in Matthew chapter 19 and also briefly referred to here in the Sermon on the Mount, is a great message for each person, especially for those who are committed to one another within the sacrament of marriage.

As we hear these words, we need to pray for God's blessing upon all of those who are married, and those who are struggling within their marriage; and for people who, in various ways, have had difficulty and pain and struggle. We need to support and to encourage people in that situation, and to ask the Lord to bless them. Let's meditate upon that, and pray that each one of us may be faithful to the Lord.

> *It was also said, "Whoever divorces his wife, let him give her a certificate of divorce." But I say to you that every one who divorces his wife, except on the ground of unchastity, makes her an adulteress; and whoever marries a divorced woman commits adultery.*

⌐

> *Again you have heard that it was said to the men of old, "You shall not swear falsely, but shall perform to the Lord what you have sworn." But I*

> *say to you, Do not swear at all, either by heaven,*
> *for it is the throne of God, or by the earth, for it*
> *is his footstool, or by Jerusalem, for it is the city*
> *of the great King.*

We are called simply to speak words of truth to one another. Throughout the scriptures, including the gospels, people swear before the Lord, especially for formal and profound commitments of life. But people can do this all the time. They can invoke the divine power and the name of God in every possible way. Our Lord says this is not right—this swearing by the throne of God, or by the earth, or by his footstool, or by Jerusalem. We are people who simply need to say, "Here I am, Lord; I come to do your will." One of the great gifts God gives to us is language; what we speak should be clear and true. We need to do what we say we will do.

In one of the psalms, we read a great testimonial paid to a man: "He keeps his word, come what may." That is the kind of commitment to a pledge to which we are called daily. Our Lord warns against always swearing oaths, as if adding the divine dimension will make our words stronger. If we are really, truly living our life faithful to the Lord, we should not need to swear oaths. Let the words we speak be the words we live. What we say, we do.

So let us reflect upon this as our Lord speaks to us:

> *Again you have heard that it was said to the*
> *men of old, "You shall not swear falsely, but shall*
> *perform to the Lord what you have sworn." But I*
> *say to you, Do not swear at all, either by heaven,*
> *for it is the throne of God, or by the earth, for it*
> *is his footstool, or by Jerusalem, for it is the city*
> *of the great King.*

Let's spend a little quiet time now and ask, "Am I a person who keeps his word, come what may?" Am I clear and transparent all the way through? Or do I live in levels? Do I have a kind of an apple-strudel life of different and conflicting levels: what I mean, what I say I mean, what I think I mean, what you think I mean? The observation "What you see is what you get" is meant as a compliment. Up front and open and candid and clear—that's the way we're supposed to be. Let's pray to the Lord that we can be simple and clear. Let's pray that we don't clutter up our lives with the complexity of swearing by the throne of God or by Jerusalem, but that we just live a life, clear and simple, true before the Lord. Let's ask the Lord's grace to do that.

⁓

And do not swear by your head, for you cannot make one hair white or black. Let what you say be simply "Yes" or "No"; anything more than this comes from evil.

Let's just be simple. We do not swear by our head because we can't turn one hair white or black. We have to lighten up a little bit. Our Lord includes this command after this very serious section of the Sermon on the Mount; he tells us, "Do not swear by your head, for you cannot make one hair white or black." So, our life is in the hands of the Lord. Let's not complicate things, but simply serve the Lord faithfully and be who we are. The same sentiments are echoed in this wonderful line spoken during the ordination of a deacon: "Receive the Gospel of Christ, whose herald you now are. Believe what you read, teach what you believe, and practice what you teach." Our life in Christ should be as simple as that. We're complicated; God is simple and straightforward.

The more we come away from the rim of complexity to the hub of simplicity, the closer we come to God.

The tradition of the Church has a great vision of the path of the spiritual life. It begins in the struggle with sin, the purgative way. The purification of sin which is like being in the outer ditches of the castle, fending off the alligators in the moat. After we're purified, we reach a greater level of simplicity, or the illumination, where we read the word of God, and let the light of Christ shine in our hearts. And finally we come to union, just being with the Lord. That is simplicity, the center of it all.

Mass is structured along the same lines: we start with the penitential, "Lord have mercy," asking God's mercy for our sins. After the confession of sin, we move into the experience of illumination through the scriptures, the light of Christ that shines in us through the word. Finally, we come to communion, to proclaim, "The body of Christ. Amen." It is the Lord: "My Lord and my God." Then we can just be, in union with our eucharistic Lord.

A famous old story tells of a person in the back of the church who was praying away without a rosary or a book, just looking up at the tabernacle. The priest asks, "What are you doing? You don't seem to have a prayer book." The parishioner says, "I look at Jesus. Jesus looks at me. And we're happy." Prayer isn't more complicated than that. It isn't rocket science. We get so caught up in creating complications, especially if we're kind of religious: we can be "checking the dials" to see how spiritual we are. There's a saying: "The unexamined life is not worth living, the unlived life is not worth examining, and the over-examined life is hell." Our Lord is telling us, "Lighten up a bit; don't get so complex, swearing by this or that or the other thing, and trying to nail it all down. No, no. Let go. Life is in the hands of the

Lord." Pope John XXIII is said to have prayed when he was going to bed: "Well, Lord, it's your Church. You take care of it. I'm going to bed."

Our Lord is teaching us very simply: don't swear by your head. You can't turn your hair white or black. Wake up. Let your answer be "yes" or "no." Be simple. Love God. Do it every day. Love your neighbor. That's it. Then we die and we see him face to face, and we don't worry about anything else.

Let's think about that simplicity and ask the Lord, "Help us to simply say 'yes' to you, O Lord, and 'no' to those things that should cause us to pluck out our eye and cut off our hand." Just say, "It's in your hands, O Lord. Speak, Lord; your servant is listening. Here I am." Just ask the Lord for that simplicity of heart, which is the great gift of holiness.

༄

Please reread the scripture passage at the beginning of the chapter (pages 35–36).

༄

Our Father

Hail Mary

Glory Be

Chapter Four

Matthew 5:38–6:6

Within this chapter we move to a new topic within the Sermon on the Mount. To accommodate nine sessions of lectio divina, I have broken the Sermon on the Mount into nine sections that don't quite follow the natural divisions of the text. The first part of the Sermon on the Mount is the Beatitudes, which we looked at and prayed in the first chapter. The second part, also in Matthew chapter 5, holds up standards that some people have felt to be almost impossible to follow: "You must be perfect, as your heavenly Father is perfect."

These standards stretch us. They take us beyond our normal desire to just be complacent and comfortable Christians. In this section, our Lord uses dramatic language to get our attention. For example, he tells us "If your hand causes you to sin, cut it off; if your eye causes you to sin, pluck it out." But I think we get the point. We need to have that kind of dramatic language in this portion of the Sermon on the Mount to shake us up, to make us think, to make us recognize that we as Christians cannot simply drift along like corks bobbing along in the stream. No, we need to live our faith to the full. And this dramatic language, which the Lord uses in this first section of the Sermon on the Mount, reminds us of that. This dramatic instruction ends midway through this chapter's selection: "Be perfect, as your heavenly Father is perfect."

Then Jesus shifts his focus and his tone. He begins to shift toward some of the daily requirements for Christians. He says that when we demonstrate our love for the Lord through prayer, fasting, and almsgiving—three great ways in which we serve the Lord as disciples—then we must be sure to do them with a pure heart. We should not do them to show off for others, but instead do them in secret where our Father sees.

In chapter 5 of the Gospel of Matthew, we finish off the dramatic introduction to the Sermon on the Mount, where those high and glorious standards are presented to us. And then as we move into chapter 6, we shift toward the way in which we disciples of Christ should engage in prayer, fasting and almsgiving.

Let us now ask the Lord to free us from any of those things that distract us, from the cares and concerns that fill our hearts and minds and get in the way of listening to the Lord God and listening to one another. So often we miss the many-splendored presence of the Lord because of our busyness and the many distractions in our head. So let's just say: Lord, help me to be at peace during this time as I hear your word. Let all of that clutter, that static within me be at peace, so that there might be a place within my heart for you, O Lord. Let this portion of scripture be your pathway to my heart.

Speak, Lord; your servant is listening.

Come Holy Spirit, fill the hearts of your faithful, and enkindle in us the fire of your love. Send forth your spirit, and we shall be created, and you shall renew the face of the earth.

Speak, Lord; your servant is listening.

Lord, help me to hear that word within the Holy Gospel that above all is what you say to me this evening, that one thing that I need most fully to reflect upon in my own life as a disciple.

You have heard that it was said, "An eye for an eye and a tooth for a tooth." But I say to you, Do not resist one who is evil. But if any one strikes you on the right cheek, turn to him the other also; and if any one would sue you and take your coat, let him have your cloak as well; and if any one forces you to go one mile, go with him two miles. Give to him who begs from you, and do not refuse him who would borrow from you. You have heard that it was said, "You shall love your neighbor and hate your enemy." But I say to you, Love your enemies and pray for those who persecute you, so that you may be sons of your Father who is in heaven; for he makes his sun rise on the evil and on the good, and sends rain on the just and on the unjust. For if you love those who love you, what reward have you? Do not even the tax collectors do the same? And if you salute only your brethren, what more are you doing than others? Do not even the Gentiles do the same? You, therefore, must be perfect, as your heavenly Father is perfect. Beware of practicing your piety before men in order to be seen by them; for then you will have no reward from your Father who is in heaven. Thus, when you give alms, sound no trumpet before you, as the hypocrites do in the synagogues and in the streets, that they may be praised by men. Truly, I say to you, they have received their reward. But when you give alms, do not let your left hand know what your right hand is doing, so that your alms may be in secret; and your Father who sees in secret will reward you. And when you pray, you must not be like the hypocrites; for they love to stand and pray in the synagogues and at the street corners, that they may be seen by men. Truly, I say to you, they have received their reward. But when you pray, go into your room and shut the door and pray to your Father who is in secret; and your Father who sees in secret will reward you.

〜

You have heard that it was said, "An eye for an eye and a tooth for a tooth." But I say to you, Do not resist one who is evil. But if any one strikes you on the right cheek, turn to him the other also; and if any one would sue you and take your coat, let him have your cloak as well; and if any one forces you to go one mile, go with him two miles.

"An eye for an eye, and a tooth for a tooth." This is the old law, which was intended to act as a moderation upon revenge, because sometimes people would respond out of proportion to the injury. And unfortunately we still see this today, where revenge and the memory of ancient wrongs can lead to terrible strife among people. And so, "an eye for an eye, and a tooth for a tooth" is the way to bring some order and proportion. This kind of reciprocal punishment is found within the gospel as well, including the Gospel of St. Matthew, where our Lord speaks of the punishment we receive for the ways we have turned away from him. At the end of the Gospel of Matthew, in the great last judgment scene, Jesus tells of the different final rewards for the sheep and for the goats.

But here in the Sermon on the Mount, our Lord is talking about our personal relationships with one another. Judgment is for the Lord God, not for you or for me. He says, "You have heard that it was said, 'An eye for an eye, and a tooth for a tooth.' But I say to you . . ." This "I say to you" says as much about who Jesus is as it says about the content of his message. He is one who can revoke and he can complete; he can fulfill that which has been said before.

"But I say to you, Do not resist one who is evil. But if any one strikes you on the right cheek, turn to him the other also; and if any one would sue you and take your coat, let him have your cloak as well; and if any one forces you to go one mile, go with him two miles."

In this passage, he calls us to this overwhelming goodness. This reminds me of a scene on the way to Calvary. The Roman soldiers grabbed Simon of Cyrene and forced him to help carry the cross. The Romans had the power to make someone do what they wanted done, such as carry their gear. Jesus doesn't ask for retaliation. Jesus says that if someone makes you go one mile, go two miles. Overwhelm the person with goodness.

Elsewhere in the sacred scriptures, of course, we are told to resist evil, to seek justice. When we read a passage of scripture, we can't simply focus in on that one section only; the reality is found in the whole picture. In many passages the Lord tells us of the necessity of justice, but in this passage he emphasizes the extraordinary goodness required of us as his disciples. As we read these words, we should think of the Lord himself. He lives out the Sermon on the Mount. On his way to Calvary, he is struck and attacked. We see all that evil coming toward him, and our natural response in that situation would be to give it right back. But our Lord takes the evil, and in return he gives love and compassion. He does not give what he gets. Often, we choose to give what we get, using "an eye for an eye and a tooth for a tooth" in our relations with one another. We can prove, with exquisite logic, how we have been offended, and how we have a right to respond. We can waste the precious time the Lord God has given us on this earth with parsing out the ways in which we have been wronged. But, judgment is the Lord's, not yours or mine.

So our Lord says, look, get out of that death spiral, in which you try to prove that you are right. Don't spend your life saying, "But you must understand; I was correct." Let's just go to another level. Jesus says, "You have heard that it was said 'An eye for an eye and a tooth for a tooth.' But I say to you, Do not resist one who is evil. But if anyone strikes you on the right cheek, turn to him the other also; and if anyone would sue you and take your coat, let him have your cloak as well; and if anyone forces you to go one mile, go with him two miles."

Overwhelm with goodness. Of course, we also need to seek justice and to do right, as we've read in other places in the sacred scriptures. Our Lord is not advising us to accept wrong because wrong is good; no, we need to fight evil; however, in this passage, Christ is dealing with the kind of bitterness that can grow within us when we start getting into a tit-for-tat relationship with others. He's saying to let that go: there's no freedom there; there's no life. This is not the way of the Lord God.

At the same time, he's not promising that if we turn the other cheek, the other person will change for the better: "Oh, I'm really impressed by that. I won't do anything now." Turning the other cheek isn't a technique for getting others to abandon evil. Turning the other cheek is what God expects of us, so that we're not drawn into imploding bitterness, this acid reality whereby we can get so focused on our rights that we lose sight of the greater context.

Let's listen to these words, and then deep within our own hearts ask, "Is there something in my life, some long-festering memory, some relationship where I'm clinging to a memory of an injustice, and it's robbing my life of joy? Are there times when I can be too nitpicky and insistent on righteousness? Are there times when I am quick to judge? Is there anything in my life to which our Lord is especially speaking in this portion of the Sermon on the Mount? What is our Lord saying to me particularly? How is he calling me to break free of that kind of narrowness that can absorb and destroy?"

> *You have heard that it was said, "An eye for an eye and a tooth for a tooth." But I say to you, Do not resist one who is evil. But if any one strikes you on the right cheek, turn to him the other also; and if any one would sue you and take your coat, let him have your cloak as well; and if any one forces you to go one mile, go with him two miles.*

Give to him who begs from you, and do not refuse him who would borrow from you.

Much like the call to turn the other cheek, this passage is a call to react with overwhelming generosity. "Give to him who begs from you, and do not refuse him who would borrow from you." Now, some ways to help a person who is asking for assistance may be more prudent or effective than others. Sometimes our giving can do damage. Jesus' point is clear, however. He says, "Loosen up. Don't cling to your possessions. You can't take them with you."

We cling to so many things, not only money. This passage probably makes most of us think of money at first. But people have a variety of needs, many of which we can address by going out of our way to give a bit of our time. How we spend our time and money are the two best measures of what's important in our lives. We must not be stingy or miserly with either of them.

We have a model here in the generosity of our Lord, who did not cling to his equality with God but gave himself totally. Give and do not count the cost. Fight and do not heed the wounds. Don't measure out life in little coffee spoons. Life is too short for that. We need to live generously, with our time, with our money, with our talents.

So, "give to him who begs from you, and do not refuse him who would borrow from you."

Let's think about that in our own lives, the ways in which we can give to those who ask us. It may not necessarily be writing a check; it might be just the way we relate to other people, having that kind of open spirit to which our Lord calls us. How in my life have I not been open? How have I

been demanding in measuring the tiniest little detail when
I am in a position where I can give time or money? Lord,
forgive me.

> *Give to him who begs from you, and do not
> refuse him who would borrow from you.*

⁓

> *You have heard that it was said, "You shall love
> your neighbor and hate your enemy." But I say
> to you, Love your enemies and pray for those who
> persecute you, so that you may be sons of your
> Father who is in heaven; for he makes his sun
> rise on the evil and on the good, and sends rain
> on the just and on the unjust. For if you love
> those who love you, what reward have you? Do
> not even the tax collectors do the same? And if
> you salute only your brethren, what more are you
> doing than others? Do not even the Gentiles do
> the same? You, therefore, must be perfect, as your
> heavenly Father is perfect.*

Here's the standard: you "must be perfect as your heavenly Father is perfect." We like to draw the line about who is
our neighbor. Remember the story of the Good Samaritan?
In this story the Samaritan loves and helps someone who is
naturally his enemy. Our Lord takes the definition of neighbor and stretches it out as far as it can go. We must love the
Lord our God with heart and mind and soul. We must love
our neighbor. These are the two great commandments. At
the end of life, we are going to be asked: Have you loved the
Lord your God with heart and mind and soul? Have you

loved your neighbor as yourself? These are the two questions on the only final exam that counts.

So we need to ask, who is my neighbor? The parable of the Good Samaritan provides an answer. I can't be narrow, loving only the people who get along with me, who think the way I think, who have undeniably wise ideas on politics, life, and everything else—because their ideas are remarkably like my own. No. Sometimes within churches, people get frustrated with those who are different from themselves, but this diversity is one of the most important features of the church. The church is not meant to be a club of like-minded people. There's nothing wrong with sharing common interests with friends—that's one of the nice things in life. But that's not what church is all about for us. We don't say, "Peace be with you because I like you." In church we offer the peace of Christ to everyone, including the ones we don't particularly like, including the ones who might be in some way our enemies. We step beyond that narrow little dividing line: you are my friend, you are not; you have earned my friendship, you have not. Our Lord says, "You have heard that it was said, 'You shall love your neighbor and hate your enemy.' But I say to you, Love your enemies and pray for those who persecute you."

If we pray for people who have hurt us in some way, we're adding love to the world. That's the only way to be. Otherwise, there's too much hatred and too much exacting measurement. Pray for people who have hurt you, "so that you may be sons of your Father who is in heaven."

God doesn't seem to discriminate. "He makes the sun rise on the evil and on the good. He sends rain on the just and the unjust." Our Lord doesn't seem to be very picky about those to whom he sends his blessings. So who are we to be so discriminating about who will be our friends, and who will not? Love even our enemies, love those people who do evil; it's the only way to truly live. If not, we just get into an endless cycle, which is ultimately destructive. It gets us nowhere.

"You have heard that it was said, 'You shall love your neighbor and hate your enemy.' But I say to you, Love your enemies and pray for those who persecute you, so that you may be sons of your Father who is in heaven; for he makes his sun rise on the evil and on the good, and sends rain on the just and on the unjust. For if you love those who love you, what reward have you? Do not even the tax collectors do the same? And if you salute only your brethren, what more are you doing than others? Do not even the Gentiles do the same?"

We don't love other people in order to get a reward. Our Lord shows us a broader vision of giving and not counting the cost. Love is not measured by human terms. He says, "Be perfect as your heavenly Father is perfect." Often we compare ourselves to other people, but our standards are too narrow. We should compare ourselves to our blessed Savior. Just look at the Blessed Sacrament and say, "Lord Jesus Christ, son of God, have mercy on me, a sinner." We should always compare ourselves to God, to the Lord Jesus, and know he loves us with all our sins. In the presence of the Lord God, all our pretensions are blown away. "Be perfect as your heavenly Father is perfect." That's the standard for all of us.

Being perfect isn't an impossible demand. One of my favorite quotes, from John Henry Newman, sums it up well:

> It is the saying of holy men that if we wish to
> be perfect, we have nothing more to do than
> to perform the ordinary duties of the day well.
> A short road to perfection. Short, not because

easy, but because pertinent and intelligible.
There are no short ways to perfection, but
there are sure ones. I think this is an instruction which may be of great practical use to
persons like ourselves. It is easy to have vague
ideas of what perfection is, which serve well
enough to talk about when we do not intend
to aim at it. But as soon as a person really
desires and sets about seeking it himself, he is
dissatisfied with anything but what is tangible
and clear and constitutes some kind of direction toward the practice of it. We must bear
in mind what is meant by perfection: it does
not mean any extraordinary service, anything
out of the ordinary or especially heroic; not all
have the opportunity of heroic acts of suffer-
ings. But it means what the word perfection
ordinarily means. By perfect, we mean that
which has no flaw in it, that which is complete, that which is consistent, that which is
sound. We mean the opposite of imperfect.
And as we know well what imperfection in
religious service means, we know by the con-
trast what is meant by perfection.

He, then, is perfect who does the work of
the day perfectly, and we need not go beyond
this to seek perfection. You do not need to
go out of the round of the day. I insist on
this because it will simplify our views and fix
our exertions on a definite aim. If you ask me
what you are to do in order to be perfect, I say
first do not lie in bed beyond the due time of
rising, give your first thoughts to God, make

a good visit to the blessed sacrament, say the angelus devoutly, eat and drink to God's glory, say the rosary well, be recollected, keep out bad thoughts, make your evening meditation well, examine yourself daily, go to bed in good time, and you are already perfect.

So, there we are. A simple way to perfection! But, seriously, the perfection discussed here is to be like God. That doesn't mean to be infinite and omnipotent; it means to have the ultimate fullness of goodness in the day-to-day life that Newman writes about. He doesn't mean doing something fancy, or going a million miles away. In our daily life, perfection means to love our enemy, to be compassionate and kind, to do what the Lord says to do in the Sermon on the Mount. It is more attainable than we realize.

> *You have heard that it was said, "You shall love your neighbor and hate your enemy." But I say to you, Love your enemies and pray for those who persecute you, so that you may be sons of your Father who is in heaven; for he makes his sun rise on the evil and on the good, and sends rain on the just and on the unjust. For if you love those who love you, what reward have you? Do not even the tax collectors do the same? And if you salute only your brethren, what more are you doing than others? Do not even the Gentiles do the same? You, therefore, must be perfect, as your heavenly Father is perfect.*

Let's reflect on that for a moment and ask the Lord to help. "Help me, O Lord, to live a life with a divine spirit—loving God and loving neighbor, without the selfish narrowness with which I can so often limit my life as a disciple of Jesus."

And now we begin a new section of the Sermon on the Mount, where our Lord speaks to us of how to pray, and how to live our life of discipleship, now that he has given us that call to glory which is found in the first section.

> *Beware of practicing your piety before men in order to be seen by them; for then you will have no reward from your Father who is in heaven. Thus, when you give alms, sound no trumpet before you, as the hypocrites do in the synagogues and in the streets, that they may be praised by men. Truly, I say to you, they have received their reward. But when you give alms, do not let your left hand know what your right hand is doing, so that your alms may be in secret; and your Father who sees in secret will reward you.*

As before, our Lord is saying: "Aim high." Don't aim low. In the previous verses, his message was, "Go for glory. Have the generosity of God. Live divinely on this earth." Here he is saying, when you give alms, "give to him who begs from you, and do not refuse him who would borrow from you." We're not to be narrow; we're to be generous—that is the glorious call of our life in Christ. But, as we see in this passage, there can be a lower motivation. We might give money so that we'll look better in the eyes of people around us. We might have one eye on the Lord and one eye on the audience. "Look at me," we think as we wave the money around and then drop it on the offering plate.

Jesus says that's the wrong motivation for generosity. The hypocrites, the ones who are putting on a show, are doing the right thing—they're being generous. But they're doing it in the streets so that they may be praised. "Truly I say to you, they have received their reward." It's important to ask why we are doing what we are doing. It is also important, however, that we not ask the question too often; we can get into the "paralysis of analysis," where we are always analyzing our motivation. We can't be always asking, "Am I giving so that people will praise me?" We have to lighten up. But the general gist of this passage is that we should try to do good, and not always look over our shoulder to see who is paying attention.

So Jesus says:

> Beware of practicing your piety before men in order to be seen by them; for then you will have no reward from your Father who is in heaven. Thus, when you give alms, sound no trumpet before you, as the hypocrites do in the synagogues and in the streets, that they may be praised by men. Truly, I say to you, they have received their reward. But when you give alms, do not let your left hand know what your right hand is doing, so that your alms may be in secret; and your Father who sees in secret will reward you.

Let us pray: "Lord, help me." Let us look in our own lives. Do I have my eyes on who is around me when I'm doing good? Or do I just let go and ask, "Lord, what is the right thing to do? Let me help those in need simply because it is right." Let's ask the Lord to help us have that free spirit of which Jesus speaks.

∽

> *And when you pray, you must not be like the hypocrites; for they love to stand and pray in the synagogues and at the street corners, that they may be seen by men. Truly, I say to you, they have received their reward. But when you pray, go into your room and shut the door and pray to your Father who is in secret; and your Father who sees in secret will reward you.*

We need to have the same approach with praying as with giving. It is to be done with an open and pure heart, not so that we might be seen by others. In our culture today, hypocrisy in this area is probably not as much a problem as it was for the Jewish people in Jesus' day. Today, people who go to a church to pray are not likely to rise higher in society; if anything, it's the other way around. But we are still too often conscious of the eyes and opinions of others.

At the beginning of the Sermon on the Mount, Jesus tells us to let our light shine. Now, he says to pray in secret. So which is true? Let your light shine, or pray in secret? And the answer is: yes, both. We can't have a wooden approach to the word of God. Yes, of course, we let our light shine. Yes, of course, we go into our room and shut the door and pray to the Father who is in secret. We need to reflect, to read, and to pray this passage again and again so that we can understand how it applies to our lives and our experiences.

"When you pray, you must not be like the hypocrites; for they love to stand and pray in the synagogues and at the street corners, that they may be seen by men." Perhaps the point is not *where* we are praying but *why* we are praying. When we do anything to impress others, to try to make a show, to pump ourselves up, then there's a problem. The more we pump ourselves up, the more hollow we are behind our pious face. That is not a natural, good, or wholesome way to live. We should do what we do for the Lord, and then not think too much about it. We shouldn't be watching to see who's watching. We also shouldn't be watching to see if we are watching too much to see who's watching—paying even more attention to ourselves! When we catch ourselves doing that, we should just laugh. Say, "Lord, help me to be a little more honest and transparent, and not so puffed up. Help me to take myself a little less seriously."

∽

Please reread the scripture passage at the beginning of the chapter (pages 51–52).

∽

Our Father

Hail Mary

Glory Be

CHAPTER FIVE

Matthew 6:7–15

This chapter's lectio divina is centered on the Our Father, the great prayer of our Lord that is right at the heart of the Sermon on the Mount. From the time when the Lord gave us this prayer, the Our Father has been at the heart of our lives as disciples of Jesus. The Our Father is rooted in the liturgy; and since the days of the early Church, Christians have prayed it liturgically three times a day. It is prayed at Morning Prayer, Evening Prayer, and of course, it's at the very heart of the celebration of the Holy Eucharist, just before communion.

The Lord's Prayer is prayed in many different ways. In addition to being an integral part of daily services and the Mass, it is one of the prayers in the rosary; it is connected to so many other prayers in our own personal life. I have often made use of this prayer when giving penance. I have been a priest now for about thirty-five years, and when I have thought of some creative penances, like three hundred push-ups or twenty laps around the church, I have usually refrained. Instead, I have said: "For your penance, just say the Our Father once. Slowly. Slowly. Think especially of the words, 'Thy kingdom come; thy will be done.' In those words is found the secret of sanctity."

"Thy kingdom come; thy will be done." That attitude is central to our whole life of discipleship. And yet as with the Hail Mary and the Glory Be and especially the Sign of the Cross, we pray the Our Father so many times that it becomes invisible to our hearts. The words become something on the lips and in the ears, but forgotten in the heart. Therefore we need to enter more and more deeply into the Our Father. So let us now prepare for lectio divina.

Let's release all those cares and concerns that interfere with our ability to hear the Lord. Let there be peace in our hearts, that we may hear him when he speaks to us.

Speak, Lord; your servant is listening.

Come Holy Spirit, fill the hearts of your faithful, and enkindle in us the fire of your love. Send forth your spirit, and we shall be created, and you shall renew the face of the earth.

Speak, Lord; your servant is listening.

When you are praying, do not heap up empty phrases as the Gentiles do; for they think that they will be heard because of their many words. Do not be like them, for your Father knows what you need before you ask him. Pray then in this way: Our Father in heaven, hallowed be your name. Your kingdom come. Your will be done, on earth as it is in heaven. Give us this day our daily bread. And forgive us our debts, as we also have forgiven our debtors. And do not bring us to the time of trial, but rescue us from the evil

*one. For if you forgive others their trespasses, your
heavenly Father will also forgive you; but if you
do not forgive others, neither will your Father
forgive your trespasses.*

Let's ask our Lord to show us one point within the Lord's
Prayer that speaks most profoundly to our hearts at this
moment of our lives.

᠀

*When you are praying, do not heap up empty
phrases as the Gentiles do; for they think that
they will be heard because of their many words.*

This verse describes the way we tend to pray: "Listen,
Lord; your servant is *speaking*." "When you are praying,
do not heap up empty phrases as the Gentiles do; for they
think that they will be heard because of their many words."
In ancient times, some people would pray a kind of magical
prayer, using many different words that would "catch" their
gods and bring them to their aid. That's not for us.

"When you are praying, do not heap up empty phrases
as the Gentiles do; for they think that they will be heard
because of their many words." It is not in many words that
we communicate with God or with one another. It is mostly
in listening and in being with the one we love. In a loving
relationship, we listen attentively and speak words that are
deep and authentic. So it must be with the Lord, and so it
must be in our prayer. We should have a heart that listens to
the Lord, and then our words will be authentic.

"When you are praying, do not heap up empty phrases
as the Gentiles do; for they think that they will be heard
because of their many words."

Let's ask our Lord to help us, in our own lives, to repent for the times we have prayed, using many words but not being authentic. Let's ask the Lord's forgiveness for the times we have talked to others with empty words. We should not speak to one another with empty words, and we should not speak to God that way. Let my life and my words be authentic. Let them be real and true.

Let's think about the words we use to pray, and ask forgiveness for the times we have been people of empty words.

> *When you are praying, do not heap up empty phrases as the Gentiles do; for they think that they will be heard because of their many words.*

～

> *Do not be like them, for your Father knows what you need before you ask him.*

Too often in our prayers we tell God what we need and give him instructions on how to make things right. We want our little projects to succeed. We need to pray a different prayer, trusting that our Father knows what we truly need even before we ask him. Jesus speaks of how the Lord God cares for the little birds of heaven and the whole of creation.

When we pray, we should not be full of empty words, trying to control God; nor should we use prayers as buttons we push to get what we want. We should simply pray out of love. We pray with a spirit of surrender. And our heavenly Father will take care of us in his providence. He will always be close to us and strengthen us. A very true old saying is that the providence of God rises before the sun. Surrender to God; do not try to use him to get what you want.

When I was responsible for formation of seminarians, I told them never to *use* the priesthood. You never use that which is of God. We thank God for the gifts he gives us. We come into his presence in prayer, but not with empty words and not trying to manipulate our heavenly Father.

Let's think of these words of our Lord. Do not be like the people of empty words, "for your Father knows what you need before you ask him." Let's spend a few moments in thanksgiving to the Lord God for his loving presence, and for his divine providence that envelops us in our daily struggles. Let's pray that we can let go of that desire for control, a control that is not ours, but the Lord's.

> *Do not be like them, for your Father knows what you need before you ask him.*

Pray then in this way: Our Father in heaven.

Now Jesus shows us how to pray: "Pray then in this way." He who is the way, the truth, and the life shows us the way of prayer. He knows. He who says, "Abba, Father," calls us to speak to the heavenly Father. We say, "Our Father in heaven." "Our" is the very first word. Not "My Father," but "Our Father." We are not little islands, separate from one another. We are brothers and sisters in the Lord, part of the family of faith, into which we enter through baptism. We always live in the reality of the community of the disciples of Jesus. "Our Father." So we cannot pray, "My Father," and forget our brothers and sisters. This community is always with us, to the end of time when we will be in the heavenly Jerusalem. We will not be twanging away on little harps on isolated clouds, each one of us having a private relationship with the

Lord. No, we will be in the New Jerusalem, the golden city coming down from heaven. The New Jerusalem comes down from heaven even now, wherever we gather together around the table of the Lord, where we live with one another in love. There the heavenly city Jerusalem is present. And there we pray always: "Our Father, who art in heaven." He is the Lord, the source of all.

Let's spend a moment thinking of the way in which the Lord God is our Father, and how whenever we pray, even when we are by ourselves, we are never alone. We are always part of the body of Christ, always part of the family of the Lord. We can never forget our brothers and sisters whenever we pray, "Our Father in heaven."

Pray then in this way: Our Father in heaven.

❧

Pray then in this way: Our Father in heaven, hallowed be your name.

"Hallowed be your name." Holy be your name. At Mass, we pray, "Holy, holy, holy Lord, God of power and might." We think back to Isaiah, and his great vision of the majesty of God in the Temple. When Moses comes in prayer, the Lord says, "Take off your shoes, for you are on holy ground." We pray, "Holy, holy is your name, O Lord." Acknowledging the majesty of God is part of prayer; we're not just talking with our buddy when we pray. But God's holiness is not contradictory to his love for us, for he does not live in icy majesty, distant from us. He is our Father in heaven, who loves us as his children—but holy is his name. The majesty of God is always at the heart of prayer. We live in adoration;

and if we recognize that, not only in our prayer but in our lives, then we will live and love the way we are meant to.

We must not be drawn aside by things that are not holy. We can so easily be distracted by and even worship what's unholy. We're not the only ones who get sidetracked; even saints can get distracted. There's a great line repeated twice at the end of the Apocalypse, where St. John mistakes what is holy and starts to worship the angel and not God. The angel says, "Deum adora": worship God. Get that straight and the rest will follow. We need to know who is holy: the Lord in majesty. And then we come before him trustingly, not in fear: "Hallowed be your name."

It is important in our life of prayer to be conscious of the indwelling presence of the Blessed Trinity. We do not need to go a million miles to find the holiness of God. This is the reason it can be so valuable to spend time in adoration before our Lord in the Blessed Sacrament. Here is the holiness of God, sacramentally present in our midst. It is in the presence of the true God that we can see the cheap little gods we worship—for what they are. So let's think of the false gods that we worship. And now think of the real God: "Holy, holy, holy Lord, God of power and might. Heaven and earth are full of your glory."

> *Pray then in this way: Our Father in heaven, hallowed be your name.*

> *Your kingdom come. Your will be done, on earth as it is in heaven.*

When we read the gospels, especially the Gospel of Matthew, we read of the kingdom of God. "Repent, for the

kingdom of God is near at hand." We hear the parables of
the kingdom. The parables teach us what the kingdom of
God is, and how it's in our midst when we are living in a
spirit of surrender to the will of God. The parables also teach
us that the kingdom of God is yet to be fulfilled. We know
we are not there yet. We pray as we struggle through this life
and this vale of tears: "Your kingdom come, O Lord." We ask
that in our own lives we might be drawn into the kingdom
of God, and that the kingdom of God may be more present
here in this world, which is laden down with so much that
is not of God.

We ourselves are the presence of the kingdom; we are
called to *be* that kingdom. We pray for the Lord to help us to
be what he's called us to be: "Your kingdom come, O Lord."
And we are confident in our Lord's presence in our lives:
"Christ has died, Christ is risen, Christ will come again."
That's what gives us hope as we pray, "Come, Lord Jesus,
come." In the midst of the struggles, we pray: "Your kingdom come." This prayer helps us to see what in this world
is not of the kingdom of God. Can it be of the kingdom of
God if people suffer such violence? Why does violence happen? Is this the way the world should be? We pray all the
time, "Your kingdom come, O Lord; let it be present in this
world of ours," and we pray for the coming of the kingdom
in all its glory. The kingdom is the standard, it is the star we
steer by; it is that which is of the Lord. All we say and do
must be oriented toward the kingdom of God. We must get
rid of those things in our lives that are not of the kingdom.

Let's consider the coming of the kingdom for a few
moments. "Your kingdom come. Your will be done, on earth
as it is in heaven. Your will be done." That spirit of surrender
is at the very heart of the Our Father and of our lives. It is
the pathway of holiness, guiding us in times of struggle. Our

Lady shows us the way when she accepts God's will in her life: "Be it done to me according to your word." She is the model who shows us how to live in the imitation of Christ. This surrender is abandonment to divine providence, and should be at the center of our life in prayer. So many things in life are unnecessary, while the kingdom is essential: "Your kingdom come. Your will be done."

These very words, "Your will be done," are used by our Lord in chapter 26 of the Gospel of Matthew, when he is praying in the garden of Gethsemane. He says, "Father, take away this cup, but thy will be done. If it is your will that I drink of this, thy will be done." In the garden of Gethsemane, our Lord Jesus himself prays the very heart of the Lord's Prayer. Yet, how often do we struggle with the things that take us away from God's kingdom: "*My* kingdom come. *My* will be done." When we focus on ourselves, we can get caught up in darkness. But that leads only to death.

"Our Father in heaven, hallowed be your name. Your kingdom come. Your will be done, on earth as it is in heaven." We pray for the kingdom of the Lord to be here on earth, but we don't make it happen. We don't fix this earth according to our own will, designing our version of the kingdom of God. The Lord can use us to build his kingdom, but only as we obey the will of the Lord. Remember, we have a Messiah, and he is not you or me. We need to surrender to the will of the Lord. We need to let go of those attitudes that get in the way. We need to realize, it's not my kingdom, it's not my will. There's a profound Christian wisdom based upon self-abandonment to divine providence, letting go, recognizing we don't have our hands on the steering wheel.

We say, "Your kingdom come. Your will be done, on earth as it is in heaven." The will of God is done in heaven; on this earth we may in our own individual ways be instruments of God's grace, letting his light shine while praying that the kingdom of God may become more present here. We do have a role. We're called to move out and win the world for Christ, always recognizing the mystery that we don't make it happen. Let's think about our role. Remember the penance I used to give for confession? Just pray the Our Father once, slowly, thinking about these words:

> *Your kingdom come. Your will be done, on earth as it is in heaven.*

ᗧ

Give us this day our daily bread.

We may not appreciate this part of the Lord's Prayer too much if our daily bread appears automatically on the table. But think of the number of people who live within a couple of blocks of where we live, and who are not sure if they are going to get daily bread. How many people in the world are not sure what they are going to eat tomorrow? "Give us this day our daily bread." We are radically dependent upon the Lord, to be sure; and we're also called to reach out and to be the hands of Christ in this world, to help those who do not have their daily bread.

Our prayers cannot always be mystically sublime. The most profound mysticism ultimately comes down to helping out, to caring, to washing dirty feet. Our Lord modeled this hands-on spirituality at the center of the first eucharist. He says that we should pray for our daily bread. We should pray for help in our most practical needs. If we're hungry, we should ask the Lord for food. If we are unemployed, we should ask the Lord to help us find work. We should ask for whatever we need to get through the day. And as disciples of our Lord Jesus, we need to share daily bread with those who do not have it. Our prayers should not become too ethereal. They should be about needs as basic as food.

Sometimes in our tradition of faith, we think of the daily bread that goes beyond simply the physical, the bread of the eucharist, which is the Lord himself. We also need that, most profoundly. We need to go deeper than simply our physical need for bread. But the physical needs are there. So let's think about that, as we hear this most basic and practical part of the Our Father, the part that addresses our hungry stomachs. We say, "Give us this day our daily bread." And as we do, let's think of our Lord's words, "When I was hungry . . . when I was in prison . . . when I was in need . . ."—and not just in need of empty words, but in real need of—what you did for the least of my brothers and sisters, you did for me." How often do I go beyond praying for my own daily bread, to ask God's help for other people? "Whatever you did to the least of these, you did for me," our Lord says to us.

Give us this day our daily bread.

~

*And forgive us our debts, as we also have forgiven
our debtors.*

So, we've prayed for our daily bread, and now we attend to our debts. Later in Matthew, to expand on this line of the Our Father, our Lord tells a parable about a man who was forgiven a big debt. The man then went out and demanded repayment from those who owed him much smaller sums. "Forgive us our debts, as we forgive our debtors." It's assumed that we ourselves are debtors, and that there are people who owe us, as well. But we have to recognize the proportion here: our Lord is so gracious to us, and so how can we be so harsh to one another? We are clear on the exact amount of what is owed to us. But in the great scheme of God's providence, what does that mean? In the mercy of God, how can we be so picky about demanding the rightful payment of debts to us, when we recognize how much we owe the Lord and how gracious he is to us? "Forgive us our debts, as we also have forgiven our debtors."

So much in life can be destroyed if we're constantly thinking of the injustices we've suffered, and not recognizing how much we ourselves are sinners. That's why it's a great thing to get to confession. I say, "Bless me, father, for I have sinned," and I confess. I acknowledge my failures and weaknesses, my debts to God and to others. The confession part of the sacrament of reconciliation is so very important. We prepare the way to receive absolution from God by saying, "Bless me, father, for I have sinned," and then we admit how we have sinned—how we are not perfect, how we don't have control over it all, how we have offended others. And it is a good practice to articulate these failings, though God doesn't need us to inform him of them. Just as our Lord says, "Your Father knows what you need before you ask him," our Father knows our sins.

This confession of sins is profoundly important so that we can recognize the fact that we are sinners. If I am truly confessing from the heart and regularly receiving the sacrament of reconciliation, then when I walk away from the confessional, and I see the person who has offended me, how can I be so demanding of that person? We're all frail, but we sometimes forget it; and so we need to get to confession regularly, and then think of the words:

*And forgive us our debts, as we also have forgiven
our debtors.*

ᖆ

*Do not bring us to the time of trial, but rescue us
from the evil one.*

The words we usually pray are: "And lead us not into
temptation, but deliver us from evil. Amen." This transla-
tion is perhaps closer to the Greek text. "Lead us not into
temptation" does not mean that God is out there tricking
us and trying to get us into trouble. It means precisely, "Do
not bring us to the time of trial." Help us, O Lord, for we
are so weak in the face of temptation. We so often fail when
we come to the time of trial. This testing can be good for us,
though whether we need it or not, we're going to be tested.
This world is a vale of tears.

We all struggle with temptations; it's part of the experience of our life. And temptation is not a sin. It's a testing. If
we fail in the test—if when probed by the situation we then
consent to evil—then that is a sin. But the testing itself is
not. The testing is part of the condition of our journey, like
turbulence on an airplane. Do not bring us to the time of
trial, but help us in the time of trial that is bound to come.
May we not be like Adam and Eve described in chapter 3
of Genesis. They were tested, and they failed because they
wanted that illusion of power and control. Instead, we strive
to imitate Christ. Remember Christ's temptation in the
desert? He resists the temptation, immediately dismisses it,
even when the devil quotes scripture. Follow the example of
Christ, rather than that of Adam and Eve.

"Do not bring us to the time of trial, but rescue us from
the evil one." The Greek words could mean "from the evil

one" or "from evil." Our usual prayer is, "Lead us not into temptation, but deliver us from evil." But the point is the same: Help! Help us, O Lord; rescue us. Remember the name of our Savior, our Rescuer, Jesus? We often use the word "savior" but it has become so religious a word that it is like a crucifix on a wall that we do not see because it is always there. We forget the meaning of "savior" which is *rescuer*. It means the lifeguard diving in to pull us out of the water when we're sinking. It means the firefighter rushing into the building to save us from the flames. That's what the name "Jesus" means; that is what a rescuer, a savior is.

So we ask our heavenly Father, "Help!" This is a good way to end the Our Father: Help! Help us, O Lord. We need you. We are so frail. Do not bring us to the time of trial, but rescue us from the evil one. For we are so very weak, and we need your help all the time. Without you we are nothing, and we need to recognize that the other people around us are very weak, too. That's why we forgive them, as we ask them to forgive us. And we're so thankful that our Lord forgives us.

So in a spirit of thanksgiving and gratitude for God's presence, let us think about our weaknesses and our Rescuer.

> *Do not bring us to the time of trial, but rescue us from the evil one.*

⁓

> *For if you forgive others their trespasses, your heavenly Father will also forgive you; but if you do not forgive others, neither will your Father forgive your trespasses.*

Our Lord repeats the point he made a bit earlier in the Our Father. And he said earlier, "Forgive us our debts, as we also have forgiven our debtors." Remember the parable of the man who was forgiven a great debt, and then did not forgive smaller debts? Jesus keeps repeating that point. I guess he knows us. He knows that we need this lesson repeated again and again to remind us that we need to be forgiving of others, because so often we are not. We ourselves are in need of forgiveness.

෴

Please reread the scripture passage at the beginning of the chapter (pages 68–69).

෴

Our Father

Hail Mary

Glory Be

CHAPTER SIX

Matthew 6:16–24

In this chapter we continue with our prayer of the Sermon on the Mount through lectio divina, hearing the words of our Lord concerning fasting. And after that we move on to reflect upon the profound question: where is your treasure in life? What is important? The setting of priorities is essential to our lives as disciples. Then we read a little bit about dealing with mammon and the things that can distract us from the Lord's pathway.

As we enter into lectio divina, let us ask the Lord to free us from all those distractions, from those things that so often can fill our hearts and leave no room for the Lord: the buzz of worry, and all those concerns that our Lord speaks about in this portion of the Sermon on the Mount.

⁓

Speak, Lord; your servant is listening.

Come Holy Spirit, fill the hearts of your faithful, and enkindle in us the fire of your love. Send forth your spirit, and we shall be created, and you shall renew the face of the earth.

Speak, Lord; your servant is listening.

Lord, help me to listen not only with my ears but with my heart to that one thing in these words that you want me to hear today, that one reality which is most important for me right now in this part of my journey of faith.

And when you fast, do not look dismal, like the hypocrites, for they disfigure their faces that their fasting may be seen by men. Truly, I say to you, they have received their reward. But when you fast, anoint your head and wash your face, that your fasting may not be seen by men but by your Father who is in secret; and your Father who sees in secret will reward you. Do not lay up for yourselves treasures on earth, where moth and rust consume and where thieves break in and steal, but lay up for yourselves treasures in heaven, where neither moth nor rust consumes and where thieves do not break in and steal. For where your treasure is, there will your heart be also. The eye is the lamp of the body. So, if your eye is sound, your whole body will be full of light; but if your eye is not sound, your whole body will be full of darkness. If then the light in you is darkness, how great is the darkness! No one can serve two masters; for either he will hate the one and love the other, or he will be devoted to the one and despise the other. You cannot serve God and mammon.

～

And when you fast, do not look dismal, like the
hypocrites, for they disfigure their faces that their
fasting may be seen by men. Truly, I say to you,
they have received their reward.

When you fast. Our Lord doesn't say, "*If* you fast." He
says, "*When* you fast," assuming that we will. Prayer, fasting,
and almsgiving are part of the rhythm of the Christian life,
part of the role of disciples. And so he says, "When you fast."
Do we fast? During Lent, we give up some food—perhaps
candy—which can be a good discipline. But what is the
purpose of this fasting? Sometimes we give a good rational
explanation for it, such as, "If I don't eat a lot of food, I
could take the money saved and give to the poor." But that's
almsgiving, not fasting. Fasting doesn't need that kind of
rational explanation to make it valuable. We need to turn
our attention to fasting itself for a moment, to see its role in
our lives, not only in Lent, but throughout the whole of our
discipleship. At penitential times and at other stages of life,
we need to think about what our Lord says here. "And when
you fast, do not look dismal, like the hypocrites, for they
disfigure their faces that their fasting may be seen by men.
Truly I say to you, they have received their reward."

When I fast, I give up something. It is not a matter of giving
up a sin—that would be repentance, not fasting. But when I
fast, I give up something good, but something to which I can
easily become a slave. As we journey through life, we so often
become consumed by the things we consume. Is a consumed
consumer all that I am? Let me think of the things in life to
which I'm enslaved. What are the things—not even sins but
good things—that can weigh me down and take up my time

and absorb my life to an unhealthy degree? These are things that I say I don't really need—I can live without them. But can I? I will find out when I fast, when I begin to let go of things, even good things, which I consume and which can consume me, taking me away from that lightness of spirit, which is the spirit of the disciple of Jesus. Prayer, fasting, almsgiving, poverty, chastity, obedience are different pathways that lead us along the life of discipleship. Let us reflect upon those words of the Lord, which talk of fasting not as an option but an expectation. "When you fast." When do I fast? From what in my life do I need to fast? What things in my life enslave me and consume me?

> *And when you fast, do not look dismal, like the hypocrites, for they disfigure their faces that their fasting may be seen by men. Truly, I say to you, they have received their reward.*

❧

> *And when you fast, do not look dismal, like the hypocrites, for they disfigure their faces that their fasting may be seen by men. Truly, I say to you, they have received their reward.*

It's assumed that we fast, that we have disciplines of prayer, disciplines of the body. We are not angels, who by definition do not fast from food. Angels are spirits; but we are incarnate, in bodies, and so we do need to fast. When we fast, we are not to look dismal like the hypocrites. When we're hypocritical, we have a mask that we want to show to others, a good side that we hope others see when we fast or do acts of goodness. Our Lord tells us, "When you fast, do not look dismal, like the hypocrites, for they disfigure their faces that their fasting may be seen by men." The hypocrites in the gospel are perhaps not enslaved to food, but they seem to want to project an image. Perhaps they are enslaved to their ego. Hypocrites look to see if people notice what they are doing. This is a temptation that can come to us not only when we fast, but throughout our whole life in Christ. Whatever good we do, the temptation is to do it in order to be seen by others. But we shouldn't be looking around for approval or trying to get ahead through our religiosity. We should simply do what is good because it is good.

Hypocrisy is the problem, our Lord says. He assumes that we fast, because fasting is letting go of those things that can so easily enslave us. It is training and freeing ourselves up, that we might more fully be disciples by this discipline. Of course, our motivation matters. We should not do any good thing, and certainly not fast, just to be seen by others. "Truly I say to you, they have received their reward." The hypocrites want to be admired, a reward that can last a few seconds, and then is gone. We know the phrase about having fifteen minutes of fame. In our spiritual lives, we can be aiming for that kind of fleeting popularity. In doing so we miss the point of fasting and doing good. In all that we do, we need to forget ourselves. Let go of the ego and of that insecurity that motivates us to look to see how we're doing. We need to be lighthearted and free. And that is, after all, one of the purposes of fasting: to free ourselves to be better disciples.

So let's listen, and as we hear these words, let's reflect on the mixed motives in our religious exercises. Ask the Lord to purify our intentions, so that we may love him and serve him for his own sake, and not simply for the advantage we might receive, or for the admiration of others. We do need to think about others, but not to impress them or seek approval for our actions. Let us ask the Lord's forgiveness for the times we have forgotten the real purpose of our fasting, and reflect upon what rewards we are seeking in life.

> *And when you fast, do not look dismal, like the hypocrites, for they disfigure their faces that their fasting may be seen by men. Truly, I say to you, they have received their reward.*

> *But when you fast, anoint your head and wash your face, that your fasting may not be seen by men but by your Father who is in secret; and your Father who sees in secret will reward you.*

The heavenly Father will reward us in the deepest of ways. The Father's reward far exceeds whatever kind of advantage we seek through religious behavior. Our religious discipline and our religious life are not to be undertaken for advancement, but because they're part of being a disciple, and should be done with the right intention.

The saints can show us the way. They take God very seriously, but they don't take themselves too seriously. This is a good attitude to emulate. If we are trying to do things just right and checking to see if people notice, then we are taking ourselves too seriously. That's not God's way. Many saints seem to have a much lighter spirit, even with a very serious life of prayer, fasting, and almsgiving, because they do it with the proper intention. We can think of light-hearted saints as, in a sense, holy hypocrites. They have a mask as well, but one behind which they hide their goodness, rather than the other way around. The Lord calls us to an honest life in which we have a very real relationship with our heavenly Father. He is our audience. What I am in the sight of God is what I am indeed. No more, no less. We need to forget everything else. We need to put blinders on, so that we just look straight ahead at the right things, and do not get distracted by the unimportant things.

"But when you fast, anoint your head and wash your face, that your fasting may not be seen by men but by your Father who is in secret; and your Father who sees in secret will reward you."

Fasting like this calls for a forgetfulness of self and a forget-fulness of appearances, with just a "naked intent unto God," as medieval English spiritual writers called it. Straight ahead for the Lord. To you, O Lord. That is the kind of abandon-ment to the will of the Lord to which we are called as we hear these words from the Sermon on the Mount. Let us ask the Lord now to help us to have that emptiness of ego and that openness to the Lord that get our intentions focused rightly, and not on distractions that are of no value.

> *But when you fast, anoint your head and wash your face, that your fasting may not be seen by men but by your Father who is in secret; and your Father who sees in secret will reward you.*

~

> *Do not lay up for yourselves treasures on earth, where moth and rust consume and where thieves break in and steal, but lay up for yourselves treasures in heaven, where neither moth nor rust consumes and where thieves do not break in and steal. For where your treasure is, there will your heart be also.*

"Do not lay up for yourselves treasures on earth, where moth and rust consume and where thieves break in and steal." That treasure laid up for ourselves speaks of anxiety. It reminds me of the parable where our Lord tells of the person who claimed, "I will build bigger barns and silos; I will pile up all my treasures." And that man hears the words, "You fool. This night your soul will be asked of you. And what is it all worth?" We pile up so-called treasures, and we spend so much of the greatest treasure doing it. The greatest of treasures is time, because out of time our life is woven. We may spend time laying up treasures that are susceptible to moths and to rust, but the moth and the rust will ultimately triumph. The things on which we spend so much of our lives—are they susceptible to moths and rust? If they are, what does that say about the quality of our lives? How are we susceptible to the moth and the rust?

So, "Do not lay up for yourselves treasures on earth, where moth and rust consume and where thieves break in and steal." Think of all the anxieties we have when we try to build up earthly treasure. Thieves can break in and steal. What can they steal? And what does that do to the rest of our lives, if we're absorbed in the fear of losing our treasure? We all travel too heavily loaded down with baggage.

In a great book on the priesthood, Archbishop Dolan tells the story of traveling as a young priest back and forth to studies. He comes to stay at a rectory halfway on the journey, with just a little suitcase. He admires the pastor who lives at the rectory, because the pastor lives such a simple life. When the young priest remarks on this simplicity, the pastor says, "Well, you've only got a little suitcase." And the young priest says, "But I'm just traveling. I'm just passing through." The old pastor replies, "And so are we all."

"Do not lay up for yourselves treasures on earth, where moth and rust consume, and where thieves break in and steal." Let's pray about that now. Are there things in my life on which I spend too much precious time, but which really are susceptible to the mighty moth or rust? And if so, why am I wasting my time? If so, Lord help me to see more clearly.

> *Do not lay up for yourselves treasures on earth, where moth and rust consume and where thieves break in and steal, but lay up for yourselves treasures in heaven, where neither moth nor rust consumes and where thieves do not break in and steal. For where your treasure is, there will your heart be also.*

Do not lay up for yourselves treasures on earth, where moth and rust consume and where thieves break in and steal, but lay up for yourselves treasures in heaven, where neither moth nor rust consumes and where thieves do not break in and steal. For where your treasure is, there will your heart be also.

The Sermon on the Mount is meant to show us what the treasures in heaven actually are, what they look like. The realities taught in the Beatitudes and the rest of the Sermon on the Mount are the treasures in heaven. The perspective on life, which we learn from Jesus, shows us what is important. We aim high, looking at the things that are not susceptible to moths and rust: loving God, loving neighbor in all the ways our Lord shows us.

In the early history of the Church, a pope demonstrated that he understood God's definition of real treasure. During a time of persecution against the Church, this pope was called on by the evil emperor to bring out the treasures from the church. The pope simply said, "Well, here we are," and showed to the emperor the poor, the sick, those in need— basically the people of the church. *People* are treasures of the Church; they are what matters.

Saints know what real treasure is. It's not the gold and silver chalices and precious metals used in the churches. You might have read about some of these saints actually melting down chalices and valuables to give to the poor. There's a time for giving away church treasures to help those in need, but we also learn from St. John Chrysostom that art and beauty has its place, too. He says that we need things that are beautiful and things that are majestic, for they are also a sign of God's goodness, since God's creation is made manifest in art and beauty. But Chrysostom also warns us that we need to keep things in proportion. The real treasure is found in our brothers and sisters, and in serving them.

Jesus says, "Lay up for yourselves treasures in heaven, where neither moth nor rust consumes, and where thieves do not break in and steal. For where your treasure is, there will your heart be also." Where my treasure is, my heart will be with it, guarding the treasure. So what draws my heart? The things susceptible to moth and rust? Are they worth it? "Where your treasure is, there your heart will be." Lord Jesus, help me to see where my treasure is. What is the pearl of great price, for which I will sell everything? Let's just reflect for a few moments now: in my own life, what is my treasure? For what will I give my everything? "Where your treasure is, there your heart will be also." Let's ask our Lord now to help us to focus on where our treasure is and should be, that our heart may follow, and be where it should be.

> *Do not lay up for yourselves treasures on earth, where moth and rust consume and where thieves break in and steal, but lay up for yourselves treasures in heaven, where neither moth nor rust consumes and where thieves do not break in and steal. For where your treasure is, there will your heart be also.*

The eye is the lamp of the body. So, if your eye is sound, your whole body will be full of light; but if your eye is not sound, your whole body will be full of darkness. If then the light in you is dark-ness, how great is the darkness!

In this passage, we perhaps see an ancient theory of the eye: instead of the eye simply receiving light from the out-side, the eye actually sends out light, like a lamp within the body. The science may not be quite accurate, but the point is clear. Our Lord shows us the meaning of being focused, of having the light within us. He gives an example: the eye is the lamp of the body, so if our eye is sound, our whole body will be full of light. A few years ago I had a distressing experi-ence, when I noticed that everything was going dark in my right eye. It is scary when darkness comes like that. For about a week I didn't know the cause. Then I learned that my retina was detaching. Finally I went in to see the doctor, and had it fixed that afternoon. The doctors got the retina back in place, and suddenly I could see again. What a difference!

"The eye is the lamp of the body. So, if your eye is sound, your whole body will be full of light; but if your eye is not sound, your whole body will be full of darkness. If then the light in you is darkness, how great is the darkness!" We need to have within ourselves that simple light, which our Lord speaks about through the image of the eye; we need to let the light shine. If a light goes out, physically there is darkness. And Jesus says, it is even more so, in the deeper reality that he's talking about: "If then the light in you is darkness, how great is the darkness!" We need to keep within our hearts and within our lives that simple burning light, the light of love, the light of truth and goodness. We need to let that light shine. And if the light that is more than even the physical goes out, then how deep is the darkness.

Let us spend time now, and ask the Lord's help, that we may live in the light, that the light may penetrate us totally, and that those things within us that darken the light of Christ may be taken away. Let's ask our Lord to help the light within each one of us be bright, and not be darkness.

> *The eye is the lamp of the body. So, if your eye is sound, your whole body will be full of light; but if your eye is not sound, your whole body will be full of darkness. If then the light in you is darkness, how great is the darkness!*

Lord, help the light within me to be bright, and take from me all those things that make it dark.

∽

> *No one can serve two masters; for either he will hate the one and love the other, or he will be*

*devoted to the one and despise the other. You can-
not serve God and mammon.*

We cannot be divided between God and mammon. Mammon is wealth, or objects, the kinds of things that rust and moths can take away. Mammon is whatever we cling to that is less than what God wants for us. "You cannot serve God and mammon." There's an old line: "Purity of heart is to will one thing." Just before talking about mammon, our Lord says, "Thy kingdom come, thy will be done." We need an undivided heart, focused on the will of God and not on our own will; focused on treasure in heaven and not on treasure on earth. Where is my treasure? What mammon draws me away, splits my intention? This division could make me that kind of hypocrite who follows God publicly on Sunday, but privately, the rest of the week, follows mammon. We must not live divided lives. We must have a heart for only one master.

The things of this world which are created by the Lord, and which are good, are meant to be used for the glory of God and the service of one another. There's nothing wrong with them in themselves. There is nothing wrong with mammon in itself, if it's used for good, and does not become the master. We always have to come back to that question: who or what is my master? We use the term "Lord" so frequently that its meaning is obliterated by repetition. We speak of our Lord Jesus as if Lord is just a name. But is he our Lord, or not? Is he our only master? That question may be enough to spend a life on. "To you, O Lord, I give my life. Not for the sake of gaining anything, not seeking a reward, but as you yourself have loved me, O ever-loving Lord."

No one can serve two masters. It's not worth it; we get ripped apart. But we try so often, keeping our own little gods on the side. Pursuing a million dollars could be our little god. That pursuit of wealth is a type of god that is obvious. There are a lot of other little gods and attractions and lords that we can have that may be far less obvious. It is easy to look at someone else and say, "Oh, there's mammon." But we need to look in the mirror, rather than through the window, and look and see in our own heart, what is mammon for us. It need not be obvious, and maybe it is more dangerous when it isn't obvious.

> *No one can serve two masters; for either he will hate the one and love the other, or he will be devoted to the one and despise the other. You cannot serve God and mammon.*

What is in my life, obvious or not so obvious, that other people may or may not know, which is most likely to be a false master, one that will take me away from our Lord? O Lord, free me from that; help me to serve you alone.

～

Please reread the scripture passage at the beginning of the chapter (page 84).

～

Our Father

Hail Mary

Glory Be

CHAPTER SEVEN

Matthew 6:25–34

This section of the Sermon on the Mount is about one thing: it is an extended treatment of the theme of worry. All of us in different ways deal with anxiety. In the very center of the Mass, we pray for protection from two things that weigh us down: "Keep us free from sin, and protect us from all anxiety, as we wait in joyful hope for the coming of our Savior Jesus Christ." Anxiety is very much a part of our lives, and it has a central place in the Lord's teaching in the Sermon on the Mount. So now we will be reflecting upon worry and what our Lord says to us about the place of worry in our lives.

~

Let's let go of all those worries, cares, distractions that can clutter up our hearts and our minds, that can make it so that we don't hear the Lord, that we don't hear one another, or even ourselves. Let go of all those things, so that we can hear the Lord who speaks in a gentle breeze, and not in the thunder and lightning.

Speak, Lord; your servant is listening.

Come Holy Spirit, fill the hearts of your faithful, and enkindle in us the fire of your love. Send forth your spirit, and we shall be created, and you shall renew the face of the earth.

Speak, Lord; your servant is listening.

Therefore I tell you, do not worry about your life, what you will eat or what you will drink, or about your body, what you will wear. Is not life more than food, and the body more than clothing? Look at the birds of the air; they neither sow nor reap nor gather into barns, and yet your heavenly Father feeds them. Are you not of more value than they? And can any of you by worrying add a single hour to your span of life? And why do you worry about clothing? Consider the lilies of the field, how they grow; they neither toil nor spin, yet I tell you, even Solomon in all his glory was not clothed like one of these. But if God so clothes the grass of the field, which is alive today and tomorrow is thrown into the oven, will he not much more clothe you—you of little faith? Therefore do not worry, saying, "What will we eat?" or "What will we drink?" or "What will we wear?" For it is the Gentiles who strive for all these things; and indeed your heavenly Father knows that you need all these things. But strive first for the kingdom of God and his righteousness, and all these things will be given to you as well. So do not worry about tomorrow, for tomorrow will bring worries of its own. Today's trouble is enough for today.

In this passage, what is the single point that our Lord speaks of, that touches me most profoundly in my life right now? What does this passage say to my head, that I might know and understand; to my heart, and to my hands? What does it call me to do in my life as a disciple?

⁓

> *Therefore I tell you, do not worry about your life, what you will eat or what you will drink, or about your body, what you will wear. Is not life more than food, and the body more than clothing?*

We all worry a lot about things. We have to, in a sense; there are matters that need our attention. But the Lord tells us not to worry! As so often in the Sermon on the Mount, the Lord gives us these extreme statements in order to shake us up, to make us think. In the story of Martha and Mary, Jesus says that Mary, who listens to the Lord and doesn't worry about preparing the meal, has chosen the better part; but without Martha, no one would have eaten. Somebody has to put the food on the table, and our Lord knows that's true. But he also knows that we do tend to worry and to lose perspective. And so he says to us, "Therefore I tell you, do not worry about your life, what you will eat or what you will drink, or about your body, what you will wear." And then he says, "Is not life more than food, and the body more than clothing?" We need to have that perspective in our lives. Obviously we have to find food and clothing and other necessities, but we can learn not to let them absorb us. "Is not life more than food, and the body more than clothing?"

"Therefore I tell you, do not worry about your life, what you will eat or what you will drink, or about your body, what you will wear. Is not life more than food, and the body more than clothing?"

Let us pray and reflect now on the ways in which we can deal with these everyday worries—such as food and clothing—with a proper sense of proportion. Let's recognize where they fit within the great scheme of things, and not be absorbed and ground down by them. So often in our life, when part of reality becomes the heart of reality, we really get in trouble, getting off-balance and concerned. We need to look at things in the right way, in their proper proportion, and then we won't be as absorbed in worry. What is more than food and clothing?

> *Therefore I tell you, do not worry about your life, what you will eat or what you will drink, or about your body, what you will wear. Is not life more than food, and the body more than clothing?*

> *Look at the birds of the air; they neither sow nor reap nor gather into barns, and yet your heavenly Father feeds them. Are you not of more value than they?*

Think of the birds flying around during springtime. They are not organized; they don't sow and reap and gather into barns, which is the way we like to organize things. And yet our heavenly Father feeds them. "Are you not of more value than they?" Again our Lord calls us to look at life with a sense of proportion—not only to look at the problems we have, which don't go away so easily, but also to situate them within the context of the whole of creation. That doesn't change the problems we face, but it puts them into perspective with the providence of God. We are in his hands, and we need to reflect upon our various issues in the context of divine providence, of the Lord who cares for the whole of creation. As we think of creation, we can remember to reflect upon the birds of the air and upon our own responsibility to care for creation as stewards of our heavenly Father.

Let us reflect now on the broader picture. Our Lord says to us, "You are all concerned with things, you who are children of God, but look at the great majesty of creation; I take care even of the birds of the air." I am reminded of Francis Thompson's great poem, "In No Strange Land":

> Not where the wheeling systems darken,
> And our benumbed conceiving soars!—
> The drift of pinions would we hearken,
> Beats at our own clay-shuttered doors.

If we look at the whole of the universe and see our own little self, we will ask ourselves why we are so caught up in all these problems.

> *Look at the birds of the air; they neither sow nor reap nor gather into barns, and yet your heavenly Father feeds them. Are you not of more value than they?*

∽

> *And can any of you by worrying add a single hour to your span of life?*

This is another way of looking at our worries. Our Lord points out the beauty of creation, but he also asks, "And can any of you by worrying add a single hour to your span of

life?" Will the worry really help anything? This is something
we need to think about, not only about worrying, but also
about a lot of other things we face. I often think of this
passage when I see people struggling with anger at another
person, being just eaten away by resentment. We understand
the many reasons for such anger, but, still, what's the point?
What benefit there enhances life? There is no benefit. All
worrying does is eat away at our own life.

Our Lord says, "And can any of you by worrying add a
single hour to your span of life?" Think of how often the
things we worry about do not even happen. I remember
a very wise person once said she had given up worrying,
because most of the things she worried about didn't happen,
and the things that did happen, she could handle. So our
Lord asks about the point of worrying. Can any of us by
worrying add a single bit to our life? If anything, worrying
may take away some of our life. The worrying can grind us
down. If we can't do anything about the problem, what's the
point of worrying about it, from just a purely practical, sen-
sible point of view? Of course worry is not usually rational. It
can get a hold of us and feed off a good imagination. We can
imagine all the things that might go wrong. But it is important just to forget, to let it all go, because worrying robs us of
the present moment. By worrying about what happened in
the past, which we can't change, and the future, which often
won't happen, we wreck the present, making our capacity to
face the future with peace much weaker.

As our Lord asks, "And can any of you by worrying add a
single hour to your span of life?" We can get so caught up in
worry, especially if we always try to think ahead. For type A
personalities, neat-desk types like me who like to plan ahead,
we often want to make everything happen in order. Then we
worry that this or that might go wrong, and begin to act as

if we are in a chess match, scanning about five moves ahead. We can fill up our lives in the present moment just by being caught up in thinking ahead. Meanwhile, something very real is destroyed: the present moment, which is the only place we actually live. Awareness of the sacrament of the present moment is central to our whole spiritual tradition. "Thy kingdom come. Thy will be done . . . Give us *this* day our daily bread," as our Lord says earlier in the Sermon on the Mount.

Let's think on these words, and think of the point of our worry. Let us think about the thing that we are most worried about right now.

Let's think of our favorite worry, a nice, rich, juicy worry. Just ask: what's the point?

> *And can any of you by worrying add a single hour to your span of life?*

⁓

> *And why do you worry about clothing? Consider the lilies of the field, how they grow; they neither toil nor spin, yet I tell you, even Solomon in all his glory was not clothed like one of these. But if God so clothes the grass of the field, which is alive today and tomorrow is thrown into the oven, will he not much more clothe you—you of little faith?*

Our Lord calls us to regard the beauty of the flowers of the field, and once again, the birds of the sky. All of creation—this beautiful gift of God—is provided for by the Lord, as he provides each one of us with life and everything within it. But if God clothes the grass of the field with such beauty—grass which is alive today and tomorrow is thrown into the oven—will he not clothe us who were made for eternity? All of this beauty of the fields is going to be chopped down and taken away and burned up. And our lives are so short as well. It's foolish to spend it worrying. Life is short; eternity is long. Tick, tick, tick—time's up.

The reality of death and its closeness to all of us is a rather grim thought. And yet death is also like the beauty of nature and the futility of worry—it is something we need to reflect upon, because it sets a proper perspective in our lives. We will be here until we are not, and then we will see the Lord face to face. The things we worry about—as the old saying goes—we can't take them with us. It's said that people on their deathbed never wish they'd spent more time in the office. This thought is a great liberator if we can only get it from the head to the heart. The people who have faced death often say that from now on they will not be worrying about all the things they used to worry about, things that once seemed so important. They finally have proportion in life.

What provides proportion is the prospect that life is short. Life is like the grass of the fields that is here today and gone tomorrow, and it's like the little bird that flies through one window and out the other side. We need to think and reflect upon the things that matter, and not upon the things that in the presence of the Lord God really are not so important. It is a good practice to bring our cares before the Lord every day in prayer and to get our minds centered on him. Spending time in adoration before our Lord in the Blessed Sacrament can help. In the presence of the eternal God, how small our worries seem. And how small are all the little things we puff ourselves up about. Lord, teach me the shortness of life, that I may gain wisdom of heart.

Let's think now on this passage. Each one of us has our own individual story, our own place on the journey, with this or that care that most preoccupies us. But we are journeying to meet the Lord, and when we see him face to face, what will that worry matter? What will really matter is how we love God and love our neighbor.

> *But if God so clothes the grass of the field, which is alive today and tomorrow is thrown into the oven, will he not much more clothe you—you of little faith?*

> *Therefore do not worry, saying, "What will we eat?" or "What will we drink?" or "What will we wear?" For it is the Gentiles who strive for all these things; and indeed your heavenly Father knows that you need all these things.*

We know that our heavenly Father knows we need these things. So we don't have to say that these things are unimportant. We do all need these things; that is not the difficulty. It is the striving and the worrying that are the problem. "Therefore do not worry, saying, 'What will we eat?' or 'What will we drink?' or 'What will we wear?' For it is the Gentiles who strive for all these things; and indeed your heavenly Father knows that you need all these things."

And so we do need things to eat, to drink, and to wear, though we should not be worn down by the burden of obtaining them. We need to plan, and we need to work, and we need to be diligent. This passage of the Sermon on the Mount would not be good for people who are lazy and don't want to do anything, because they say, "Aha, the Lord said don't worry." As with any kind of preaching of the Lord, we have to keep it in balance; not every homily—which is really what this is—can say everything at once.

We do need to work. We do need to try to find clothing and food and the rest. But it is the striving for them that kills us. It's that obsession, the thought that if we don't do it, everything is going to fall apart. No, our heavenly Father knows that we need all these things. We need to get perspective, to work for these necessities in a way that is not spiritually destructive. None of us is God. The original sin was an attempt to try to control every tree in the garden. We live in the providence of God. We need to work diligently as he calls us to do, and as he called our first parents to tend the garden. But we are not the master. We are just servants. And so we can let go, and not feel we have to have everything under our control, because God has everything under control.

> *Therefore do not worry, saying, "What will we eat?" or "What will we drink?" or "What will we wear?" For it is the Gentiles who strive for all these things; and indeed your heavenly Father knows that you need all these things.*

> ᴄ

> *But strive first for the kingdom of God and his righteousness, and all these things will be given to you as well.*

"Strive first for the kingdom of God, and his righteousness." The kingdom of God. "Thy kingdom come; thy will be done." This instruction means that we can't just drift along, letting everything unfold as it will. We do need to strive—but only for the kingdom of God and his righteousness—for things that truly matter. We need to give our whole lives to that which is the center, and not to what's on the edge. "Strive first for the kingdom of God and his righteousness, and all these things will be given to you as well." These things, such as food and clothing, are part of life; they will come. But meanwhile we need to have our hearts centered on what matters.

Let's think about that now. In my life how often do I strive for things that are not worth striving for, worrying about what will happen if I don't? Can I instead strive, deeply, in a spirit of trust, and give my whole life for the kingdom of God and his righteousness? The Lord will take care of all the other things that follow from that.

> *But strive first for the kingdom of God and his righteousness, and all these things will be given to you as well.*

⁓

> *So do not worry about tomorrow, for tomorrow will bring worries of its own. Today's trouble is enough for today.*

I remember seeing a cartoon of an office. A man is sitting at a desk, and this ugly head is coming up by the side of the desk. The man comments: "No sooner do we solve one problem but another raises its ugly head." Our Lord doesn't end his lesson on worry with, "Have a nice day"; he says, "Do not worry about tomorrow, for tomorrow will bring worries of its own." He seems to be giving us another angle to help put our worries into perspective: one thing at a time. He says, "Don't worry about tomorrow," because we don't know what changes tomorrow will bring. So let's not get caught up in that. Focus on today. Jesus prays earlier in the Sermon on the Mount, "Give us this day our daily bread," which is the proper attitude. He says do not worry about tomorrow, because it hasn't happened yet, and it is going to have its own problems. In this life we will never reach some kind of a grand plateau where we don't have worries and cares. Today's trouble is enough for today. Take one day at a time.

The great book *Abandonment to Divine Providence,* by Jean-Pierre de Caussade, talks of the "sacrament of the present moment," of God's care for us every moment of the day. We just have to pray, "Thy kingdom come; thy will be done, O Lord." My dad used to say, "Do the best you can with what you've got where you are." And then flick out the light, go to bed, and put it in the hands of the Lord. And I remember reading about Franklin Roosevelt, who of course had many problems to handle. He would say to himself at the end of the day, "Well, fellow, you've probably done as well as you could. So forget about it and start again tomorrow." The past we cannot change. The future hasn't happened. And the imaginary future that we worry about probably won't happen at all. All we have is today. This moment. And if we live it rightly, loving God and loving neighbor, then we will not regret the past and we need not fear the future. Just one day at a time in the presence of the Lord.

> *So do not worry about tomorrow, for tomorrow will bring worries of its own. Today's trouble is enough for today.*

❧

Please reread the scripture passage at the beginning of the chapter (page 98).

❧

Our Father
Hail Mary
Glory Be

CHAPTER EIGHT

Matthew 7:1–12

Let us now place ourselves in the presence of the Lord. Let all the things that distract us and occupy our hearts and minds disappear, as we say:

Speak, Lord; your servant is listening.

Come Holy Spirit, fill the hearts of your faithful, and enkindle in us the fire of your love. Send forth your spirit, and we shall be created, and you shall renew the face of the earth.

Speak, Lord; your servant is listening.

Judge not, that you be not judged. For with the judgment you pronounce you will be judged, and the measure you give will be the measure you get. Why do you see the speck that is in your brother's eye, but do not notice the log that is in your own eye? Or how can you say to your brother, "Let me take the speck out of your eye," when there is the log in your own eye? You hypocrite, first take the log out of your own eye, and then you will see clearly to take the speck out of your brother's eye.

*Do not give dogs what is holy; and do not throw
your pearls before swine, lest they trample them
under foot and turn to attack you. Ask, and it
will be given you; seek, and you will find; knock,
and it will be opened to you. For every one who
asks receives, and he who seeks finds, and to him
who knocks it will be opened. Or what man of
you, if his son asks him for bread, will give him a
stone? Or if he asks for a fish, will give him a serpent? If you then, who are evil, know how to give
good gifts to your children, how much more will
your Father who is in heaven give good things to
those who ask him! So whatever you wish that
men would do to you, do so to them; for this is
the law and the prophets.*

Let us spend a moment reflecting on these words of our
Lord. What is the one thing he says in this passage that most
touches my life where I am right now?

*Judge not, that you be not judged. For with the
judgment you pronounce you will be judged,
and the measure you give will be the measure
you get.*

Often we set ourselves up as judges to evaluate the people
around us. The Lord says, "Judge not, that you may not be
judged." For the Lord God, our heavenly Father, is the judge
of all, and we must recognize our frailty. We are not God;
we are simply servants, beloved children of the Lord. How
easily we rush in to be critical of others. We need to judge
sometimes, in the sense of looking with a discerning eye,

"seeing what is there." In the spirit of the Young Catholic Worker movement, we must "see, judge, and act." Our Lord himself shows us the way throughout the gospels, including in the Sermon on the Mount. But he also says to us, "Judge not, that you be not judged." We should not be judgmental, setting ourselves up to analyze meticulously the behavior of the people around us.

"For with the judgment you pronounce you will be judged, and the measure you give will be the measure you get." Our Lord speaks to us on this issue in the parables as well: we are not to be so harsh and cruel toward the people around us. I have already mentioned the servant who was forgiven a huge debt and then was harsh to his fellow servants who owed him much less. "Judge not, that you be not judged." We are not to set ourselves above our neighbor and pass judgment. For one thing, we don't really have time for that. Each one of us is doing so many things wrong, we probably should not have time left over to be analyzing the faults of our neighbors. On the other hand, we know that it is much more fun analyzing others than analyzing our own faults!

Notice how Jesus says, "For with the judgment you pronounce you will be judged." We are often most irate at those faults in our neighbor that are the very ones that we secretly dislike the most in ourselves. It is much easier to see those faults in other people and to vent our indignation at them. But what a sour way to go through life! When we spend time on harsh personal assessment, and when we weigh people around us and find them wanting, how can we advance the Gospel of Christ? How can we bring the joy of the Gospel to others if we always have a harsh attitude? And yet this censorious attitude is a strong temptation for each of us, and maybe especially for religious people, for those who are trying hard to do what is right. We notice that others don't seem to be trying as hard as we are; and we can become critical of them. Their flaws become so obvious to our own eyes.

We do not have time for judgment, in this short life of ours. We need all the time in our life just to repent of our own sins. We don't have any time left to meticulously analyze the sins of the people around us, the sins that are so much easier to see than our own. So our Lord speaks to us. Let us reflect on these words of our Lord.

How have I been judgmental in my life? Is there some situation in my life right now where I am focusing on the faults of the people around me? Why am I doing that? The question is not the tactical one of whether we are seeing the faults of others correctly; the question is a strategic one of "Why are we doing that? What's the point in the great scheme of things?"

Let's ask the Lord's forgiveness for those times that we have not been attentive to his words.

> *Judge not, that you be not judged. For with the judgment you pronounce you will be judged, and the measure you give will be the measure you get.*

↝

> *Why do you see the speck that is in your brother's eye, but do not notice the log that is in your own eye? Or how can you say to your brother, "Let me take the speck out of your eye," when there is the log in your own eye? You hypocrite, first take the log out of your own eye, and then you will see clearly to take the speck out of your brother's eye.*

"Why do you see the speck that is in your brother's eye, but you do not notice the log that is in your own eye?" The answer is that probably we are not going to confession enough. Seeing the speck in someone else's eye is easy enough; we are good at looking around and analyzing others' faults. But if we do not notice the logs that are in our own eyes—pride, anger, envy, greed, laziness, lust, gluttony, and those things that can darken the light of Christ within us— perhaps it is because we do not every day say, "Lord Jesus Christ, Son of God, have mercy on me a sinner."

A good practice at the end of each day is to review the day and thank the Lord God for the graces he has given to us. Then we should look at the logs that are in our own eyes, the things that we do wrong. After repenting for our logs, perhaps we will be less inclined to look at those things that others do that really are specks. We open confession with, "Bless me, father, for I have sinned. Bless me, father; help me to be forgiven the logs in my own eye. I have sinned." We don't say, "My neighbor has sinned." One of the great fruits of a daily examination of conscience, and one of the great fruits of the regular reception of the sacrament of reconciliation, is not only that we are freed of our sins and given new life, but that we can see more clearly our own frailty and faults and responsibility. If we see those failings, perhaps we can have more compassion for the people around us whose faults are very easy to see. We need to be like horses with blinders on, that look straight ahead and do not waste time getting distracted to the right and the left.

"Why do you see the speck that is in your brother's eye, but do not notice the log that is in your own eye?"

We need to think about these words and ask the Lord's forgiveness. We need the gift of proportion in our lives, so that we may recognize how often we become obsessed with the faults of others and distracted from reflecting upon what is more important: our own repentance for our own sins. Let's ask the Lord's forgiveness now for the times that we have been too observant of the sins of others and too blind to our own sins.

> *Why do you see the speck that is in your brother's eye, but do not notice the log that is in your own eye? Or how can you say to your brother, "Let me take the speck out of your eye," when there is the log in your own eye? You hypocrite, first take the log out of your own eye, and then you will see clearly to take the speck out of your brother's eye.*

⌇

> *Or how can you say to your brother, "Let me take the speck out of your eye," when there is the log in your own eye? You hypocrite, first take the log out of your own eye, and then you will see clearly to take the speck out of your brother's eye.*

We can disguise our arrogance and our harshness in an attitude of false helpfulness: "Look at all those sins of the people around me. I really must help them to get rid of their sin. Let me help you to get rid of that speck in your eye. I'm just doing it out of the noblest of motives. Let me solve your problems and everyone else's; let me reveal to you your sins and faults and the way to the Lord. For, of course, it is that which I am most deeply concerned about." And all the while we are caught up in illusion. Our real motive is simply to be arrogant and obsessed with the sins of others, so that we can be distracted from what we really should be doing, which is saying "Lord Jesus Christ, son of God, have mercy on me a sinner." We can cover our nosiness and our censorious attitude with a sheen of caring, noble motives, and intentions.

That's why every day we need to say, "Lord, show me my heart. Show me the motivation within me." Sometimes a friend, or a spiritual director, or a confessor might say to us, "Oh I see you're deeply engaged in reforming the world. Well, good for you. But maybe let's start with a little home territory first." We find that it is much more enjoyable to reform the world "out there" than to worry about the world "in here." Not only do we see the faults outside us more easily, but it gives us something of a "glow" to be a reformer of others. In our self-righteousness, we feel so justified in telling others what God teaches: "thus says the Lord." The words, "thus says the Lord," are the words of a prophet, but there's only a millimeter of difference between fidelity as a prophet and arrogance, when we forget that the Lord is the Lord, and we are not.

We have to have a humble spirit. If we're engaged in the work of the Lord—proclaiming his Gospel, or seeking to serve him faithfully in our daily life—we need all the more to lead a repentant life. According to an ancient tradition, before ordination, the candidate and the ordaining bishop pray the seven penitential psalms. When persons receive the grace of ordination, or make a religious profession, they prostrate themselves on the ground, to acknowledge that God is God and they are not. All of us need to look in the mirror every day and say, "God is God and I am not." If we can accept that reality, then perhaps that supremely exalting experience—and deadly one, too—of reforming the lives of the people around us will give way to a humble desire to repent. And we can hear these words: "How can you say to your brother, 'Let me take the speck out of your eye,' when there is the log in your own eye? You hypocrite. First take the log out of your own eye, and then you will see clearly to take the speck out of your brother's eye."

Sometimes we do have to look at the faults and sins of others because it is our responsibility, maybe because of our position within our family, or within our community. When we do have a responsibility from the Lord to look at the faults of others and to help the whole community be more wholesome by attending to that which is wrong, we need especially to ask the Lord's forgiveness for our sins. The history of the Church has good examples of great saints who had offices of responsibility to correct other people. I think of Ignatius Loyola and Don Bosco. In their writings, they mention that they might have to rebuke someone. But always, they begin by spending time in prayer and repentance, so that when they fulfill that mission to rebuke someone, they take no delight in humiliating or hurting the person. Above all we must ask ourselves, "What is my motivation in attending to what is wrong? And how am I doing it? Am I doing it as one who is conscious of the pain that it's causing the other person? And am I doing it in a way that brings life? And have I prayed to the Lord that all my own ego may be drained from this, so that this may be done with integrity, for the good of all, but without any of the hypocrisy that our Lord speaks about in this passage in the Sermon on the Mount?"

> *Or how can you say to your brother, "Let me take the speck out of your eye," when there is the log in your own eye? You hypocrite, first take the log out of your own eye, and then you will see clearly to take the speck out of your brother's eye.*

❧

Do not give dogs what is holy; and do not throw
your pearls before swine, lest they trample them
under foot and turn to attack you.

"Do not give dogs what is holy." I think our Lord is not talking here about cute little puppies. In the world of the New Testament, dogs were seen as ferocious; they were a negative symbol. "And do not throw your pearls before swine." Remember that our Lord compares the kingdom of God to the pearl of great price, for which one must sell everything. It is the great treasure. And then he tells us why we shouldn't throw pearls before swine: "lest they trample them under foot and turn to attack you." What is our Lord saying to us in these words? He's warned us not to be harsh to the people around us, even those in our society who are doing wrong. We do not sit on the throne of God, so we must hold back from that distorted tendency to be judgmental. But I think that here he reminds us that the world in which we live is not always benign. We sometimes need to have caution in the way in which we relate to the world around us. We need to be careful of the great pearl of our faith, the great pearl of the kingdom of God. As Jesus says elsewhere, we are to be as innocent as doves, but also wise. Earlier in the Gospel of Matthew, he tells us to be more gentle; but now he provides a balance, warning us to be a bit cautious, for this is a dangerous world, and it is one where sometimes the pearl of great price can be trampled and lost.

Do not give dogs what is holy; and do not throw
your pearls before swine, lest they trample them
under foot and turn to attack you.

Ask, and it will be given you; seek, and you will find; knock, and it will be opened to you. For every one who asks receives, and he who seeks finds, and to him who knocks it will be opened.

This is one of Jesus' great invitations to prayer. Of all the different forms of prayer—the prayers of adoration, repentance, thanksgiving—probably the most basic meat-and-potatoes form of prayer is asking for help. It's not the most noble; it is not sublime adoration, but it is a recognition of our dependence upon the Lord. It has its dangers: for example, we can distort prayer by using it as a button to push to manipulate life.

Ask, and you shall receive. This instruction needs to be treated with some nuance. I was a chaplain at a Catholic high school and led prayers before football games against another Catholic high school. One of the high schools was called Cathedral and the other was Bishop Ryan. Of course we didn't know whether the next day the headlines would read, "Cathedral Crushes Bishop Ryan," or "Bishop Ryan Demolishes Cathedral." Both teams prayed before the game, which might put the Lord God in a bit of a pickle. And so we would pray, but not really for success in the game. Jesus did not say, "Ask and you shall receive the victory you want." We would always pray that it would be a good and safe game, and that everyone would have fun.

When our Lord says, "Ask, and it will be given to you; seek, and you will find; knock, and it will be opened to you," we need to respond in a spirit of trust in the Lord, saying, "Thy kingdom come, thy will be done. Not my will be done, but thy will be done. But, Lord, I do have a need; help me,

Lord." What better form of prayer can we have? It's not as noble as adoration, perhaps, and not as selfless as thanksgiving, and not as sublime as repentance. But we acknowledge our reliance on God and on his power to save us. When we pray for intentions, it's a basic, simple, humble way of saying, "Help me, Lord." We don't always pray to the Lord for ourselves; it is good to pray for other people, asking the Lord to bless them. Praying the mysteries of the rosary can be beneficial for our own spiritual life, but we can also pray the rosary, saying a Hail Mary for other people. Ask, and you shall receive. Seek, and you shall find.

We must not play games with God, and God does not play games with us. With one another we do this maneuvering and positioning to ask and seek and get our way, but that's something for which we need to repent. The Lord, however, says, "Come to me as a little child." Approach the Lord without all the spin that we can put onto our desires and requests. He simply says, "Ask, and it will be given to you; seek, and you will find; knock, and it will be opened to you. For everyone who asks receives, and he who seeks finds, and to him who knocks, it will be opened." Sometimes what we receive will come in a way that we don't expect. Then we can discover that the hand of God is there, guiding and shaping our life, and what we truly need comes to us always. So we should not hold back from that simple childlike, "Help me, Lord." That spirit of surrender to the will of God is at the heart of who we are as his disciples.

Let us pray to the Lord for a spirit of simple, humble neediness and trust. Perhaps at this time we can ask the Lord for something that we need, just as a child would ask a parent.

Ask, and it will be given you; seek, and you will find; knock, and it will be opened to you. For

every one who asks receives, and he who seeks
finds, and to him who knocks it will be opened.

⌒

Or what man of you, if his son asks him for
bread, will give him a stone? Or if he asks for
a fish, will give him a serpent? If you then, who
are evil, know how to give good gifts to your chil-
dren, how much more will your Father who is in
heaven give good things to those who ask him!

When we pray, we discover ourselves. We discover our
needs. But most of all we discover God. We discover and
recognize the loving presence of our heavenly Father. And
so, whatever form of prayer we pray, whether it be adoration
or thanksgiving or repentance, or petition, whenever we pray
we discover the Father, and when we ask for bread, he will
never give us a stone. In that relationship of prayer, we ask
our loving Father with a humble spirit and a childlike openness that we may discover in different ways how he responds
to our prayer. Whatever happens, we will certainly discover
him. We come to him that way, because we know him to be
our loving Father.

Or what man of you, if his son asks him for
bread, will give him a stone? Or if he asks for
a fish, will give him a serpent? If you then, who
are evil, know how to give good gifts to your chil-
dren, how much more will your Father who is in
heaven give good things to those who ask him!

∽

So whatever you wish that men would do to you, do so to them; for this is the law and the prophets.

We read here the Golden Rule: do unto others as you would have them do unto you. A number of pagan and non-religious cultures have upheld this guideline as human wisdom and common sense. It can even be a substitute for faith, a kind of a secular morality. But our Lord doesn't say that this is just common sense. He says, "Whatever you wish that men would do to you, do so to them; for this is the law and the prophets." You shall love the Lord your God with heart and mind and soul. You shall love your neighbor as yourself. These are the two great commandments, not the Golden Rule. The Golden Rule simply leads us deeper into that profound truth of the law and the prophets.

I remember once when I was driving I saw in a little village a sign that read: "Doing good is my god." No, God is my God. Mother Teresa said, "Do something beautiful for God," not just, "Do something beautiful." Basic to the Golden Rule, the whole motivation behind it and context for it for us Christians, is the reality of our loving Father. The part of this rule that is human wisdom—whatever you wish that people would do to you, do so to them—makes human sense. But it's more than that. The rule comes with the added awareness of the presence of our loving Father: "For this is the law and the prophets."

So whatever you wish that men would do to you, do so to them; for this is the law and the prophets.

∽

*Please reread the scripture passage at the beginning of the chapter
(pages 111–112).*

∽

Our Father

Hail Mary

Glory Be

CHAPTER NINE

Matthew 7:13–28

This chapter ends our meditation upon the Sermon on the Mount, the wonderful, profound, challenging, and enlivening Sermon on the Mount, in which our Lord comes to us, speaks to us, and helps us to be his faithful disciples. Let me encourage you to continue the practice of lectio divina, entering into the word of God, praying, "Speak, Lord; your servant is listening," so that you can encounter our Lord in the words of sacred scripture. This should become a regular habit of ours, to read the scriptures prayerfully, slowly—even to read passages so often that we memorize them. Remember: what is in the book is like money in the bank, but what's memorized in our head is like cash in the pocket.

∽

Let us now let go of all those cares and concerns that so distract us. Let us ask the Lord's forgiveness for the sins we have committed, which harden our hearts and prevent us from listening to one another and listening to the Lord, for our hearts are so full of things that are not of God.

Speak, Lord; your servant is listening.

Come Holy Spirit, fill the hearts of your faithful, and enkindle in us the fire of your love. Send forth your spirit, and we shall be created, and you shall renew the face of the earth.

Speak, Lord; your servant is listening.

⌒

"Enter by the narrow gate; for the gate is wide and the way is easy, that leads to destruction, and those who enter by it are many. For the gate is narrow and the way is hard, that leads to life, and those who find it are few. Beware of false prophets, who come to you in sheep's clothing but inwardly are ravenous wolves. You will know them by their fruits. Are grapes gathered from thorns, or figs from thistles? So, every sound tree bears good fruit, but the bad tree bears evil fruit. A sound tree cannot bear evil fruit, nor can a bad tree bear good fruit. Every tree that does not bear good fruit is cut down and thrown into the fire. Thus you will know them by their fruits. Not every one who says to me, 'Lord, Lord,' shall enter the kingdom of heaven, but he who does the will of my Father who is in heaven. On that day many will say to me, 'Lord, Lord, did we not prophesy in your name, and cast out demons in your name, and do many mighty works in your name?' And then will I declare to them, 'I never knew you; depart from me, you evildoers.' Every one then who hears these words of mine and does them will be like a wise man who built his house upon the rock; and the rain fell, and the floods came, and the winds blew and beat upon that

*house, but it did not fall, because it had been
founded on the rock. And every one who hears
these words of mine and does not do them will
be like a foolish man who built his house upon
the sand; and the rain fell, and the floods came,
and the winds blew and beat against that house,
and it fell; and great was the fall of it." And
when Jesus finished these sayings, the crowds were
astonished at his teaching, for he taught them as
one who had authority, and not as their scribes.*

Spend a moment of prayer reflecting on what is in this
passage, the conclusion to the Sermon on the Mount. What
one saying of our Lord, what one message, speaks most
deeply to me in my own heart right now, in the place where
I am on the journey of life? Let me pray to the Lord that I
may listen to that message and act upon it.

⌒

*Enter by the narrow gate; for the gate is wide
and the way is easy, that leads to destruction,
and those who enter by it are many. For the gate
is narrow and the way is hard, that leads to life,
and those who find it are few.*

We're given two ways here, from deep within the tradition
of scripture and the spiritual tradition of the Church. At the
end of the book of Deuteronomy, we see the way to life, if we
love the Lord our God with heart and mind and soul; or the
way to death, if we do not. We are given a choice. We always
have choices in life; the choices are sometimes dramatic, but
more often our lives are woven out of little choices. And so
the Lord says, "Enter by the narrow gate; for the gate is wide

and the way is easy that leads to destruction, and those who enter by it are many." We do tend to have defective steering; we go off the road very easily. We often can be attracted to those things that lead us astray. So easily do we slip aside and so difficult is it for us to enter the narrow gate, to take up our cross, to deny ourselves, and to follow Christ. But our Lord says, "Enter by the narrow gate; for the gate is wide and the way is easy that leads to destruction, and those who enter by it are many. For the gate is narrow and the way is hard that leads to life, and those who find it are few."

We need to pay attention to this challenge in our own lives, and to acknowledge how often we can simply go toward those things which may seem to be easy, but which in the long run are deadly. Our Lord calls us here to the discipline of a disciple, to fidelity. We are not called to fickly follow those things that are the simplest, the wide and easy way, but to follow the way which involves sacrifice and the giving of self. "Greater love than this no one has than to lay down one's life for one's friend." Our Lord himself took the narrow path. He achieved brief worldly success, but then pioneered the way to glory by the way of Calvary.

Those two ways are before us. Like the observation in the opening of the early Christian writing, *The Teaching of the Twelve Apostles*—there are two ways: the way to life and the way to death, and there is a great difference between them. The way to life is more difficult. It challenges us not to simply feed our egos. The way to death can seem so easy, though it is an illusion, like the mirage that seems to be a lifesaving, life-giving source of water in the middle of the desert, but disappears when you approach it. So often our lives can be wasted in chasing after mirages. We need these sharp words of the Lord as he comes to the end of the Sermon on the Mount to say that there are two ways: the way to life and the way to death. We must make the choice every day, and choose that which is life giving, not that which merely is simple and easy to follow.

We're not meant to be like corks bobbing along the river just going with the flow, though in our society it is very easy to do that. It has always been so. It's no more difficult to lead a good Christian life now than it used to be. In this passage from the Gospel of Matthew, written around AD 30, long before all the various technological problems we face, the Lord Jesus said these words. They were relevant then and they are as relevant now; we need to think of today and apply his words in our own lives.

What choices am I making? What little choices do I make daily in which I need to attend to these words? What big choice do I have before me, where I need to listen to these words?

> *Enter by the narrow gate; for the gate is wide*
> *and the way is easy, that leads to destruction,*
> *and those who enter by it are many. For the gate*
> *is narrow and the way is hard, that leads to life,*
> *and those who find it are few.*

⮌

> *Beware of false prophets, who come to you*
> *in sheep's clothing but inwardly are ravenous*
> *wolves.*

"One may smile and smile and be a villain," said Shakespeare. We can have false prophets who speak, and speak convincingly, but they are like ravenous wolves in sheep's clothing. We need to be astute and aware. We need to be so centered in the presence of the Lord that we will be able to tell if that smiling, attractive message is real or false. We need to use our heads, because the good Lord gave us our minds to sort the villains from the true prophets.

Some popular writing does a particularly good job of analyzing some of the foggy thinking and the false prophets of our day. The books by Peter Kreeft are valuable in helping us discern. Socrates can be a good model; he speaks to a person and analyzes very clearly and simply where things go wrong and where things are clear. We must beware of false prophets. By definition, a false prophet comes as a prophet, as someone who seems to be speaking what is true and good. But a prophet needs to speak with integrity. It is so easy to get caught up in all kinds of enthusiasms for new ideas, but then we can lose our way.

> *Beware of false prophets, who come to you in sheep's clothing but inwardly are ravenous wolves.*

Let's spend a moment now of prayer, asking the Lord's guidance in our own lives and thinking of the times in our life when perhaps we have foolishly gone after what seemed so attractive at the time; and yet we didn't think it through enough. We didn't pray enough. We were perhaps too filled with fog to see that this was just glitz and illusion, a false prophet, a wolf in sheep's clothing. And let's ask God's forgiveness for the times we have been false prophets to others, when we have not really given honest and fair guidance to those who trust us, but have been people who have let others down. We are all frail, and we need the Lord's forgiveness, which he always gives to us.

⌐∼

You will know them by their fruits. Are grapes gathered from thorns, or figs from thistles? So, every sound tree bears good fruit, but the bad tree bears evil fruit. A sound tree cannot bear evil fruit, nor can a bad tree bear good fruit. Every tree that does not bear good fruit is cut down and thrown into the fire. Thus you will know them by their fruits.

We have all seen situations where someone is smiling and friendly, but spreading poison and division in the community. Hate begins to grow and friends begin to fight one another. That cannot be good. By their fruits you shall know them, our Lord says. Our Lord reminds us to look at their fruit, not just their words; words can be faked. We must get at the reality. And sometimes, that takes time.

Is a sheet of ice on a lake an inch thick or twenty feet thick? You can't tell very easily from the surface. It's not always safe to stomp on it to find out. But eventually, with time, we can begin to see the truth. Abraham Lincoln is believed to have said, "You can fool all of the people some of the time, and some of the people all of the time, but you can't fool all of the people all of the time." This is a good thing that people won't be fooled all the time. We need to think clearly about people and situations in our civic world, in parish communities, in families, and in the workplace, and we need to be able to sense what is real. We need to be able to answer the question: "Is this something that is truly from the Lord, or is this something destructive?"

One of the best things our Lord says here is that a little time can often tell. We shouldn't make a quick decision: it is good to let things—good or bad—have time to surface. Fruit takes a while to grow, and only when they are ripe can we judge whether they are bitter or good. Patience in discernment is especially valuable when we are responsible for a community. Gregory the Great wrote a book called *The Pastoral Care*. It's a fabulous book for this kind of spiritual wisdom—sensing in a community what is real, and what is not. He follows the words of our Lord in the Sermon on the Mount.

Let's just think within our own world, and our own life, about the need to let time reveal whether the fruits are good or not. Sometimes we don't have a lot of time to make decisions. But it's always better, if possible, to leave time to show what is real. Our Lord says elsewhere to let the weeds and wheat grow together, and then eventually it is possible to separate the weeds from the wheat. It's not always easy to see the difference right away. A little time is needed. So we should thank the good Lord for the gift of time.

> *You will know them by their fruits. Are grapes gathered from thorns, or figs from thistles? So, every sound tree bears good fruit, but the bad tree bears evil fruit. A sound tree cannot bear evil fruit, nor can a bad tree bear good fruit. Every tree that does not bear good fruit is cut down and thrown into the fire. Thus you will know them by their fruits.*

Lord, help each one of us to be clear all the way through, so that what we say and what we do are one; and that the fruits of our lives and the words of our lips are one, with no division.

Let's reflect upon our own fruits in this life, and how close they are to the words of the gospel.

~

Not every one who says to me, "Lord, Lord," shall enter the kingdom of heaven, but he who does the will of my Father who is in heaven. On that day many will say to me, "Lord, Lord, did we not prophesy in your name, and cast out demons in your name, and do many mighty works in your name?" And then will I declare to them, "I never knew you; depart from me, you evildoers."

Receive the Gospel of Christ, whose heralds we all are. Believe what we read, teach what we believe, and practice what we teach. We should say, "Lord, Lord." It's what we do when we pray. But it's not enough *only* to say, "Lord, Lord." We need to let the words of our lips go before us, and the deeds of our lives follow them. We make the Sign of the Cross on our forehead that we might know the words of the Gospel, on our lips that we might speak them, and then on our heart that it may be in harmony with them—that we may be what we proclaim. What we proclaim in the Gospel is in fact so often, too often, more than what we are. In a sense that makes us hypocrites. Or it simply makes us repentant disciples. We say, "Lord, Lord," but our Lord says that the words are not enough by themselves. Even if we prophesy and do mighty works in his name, if our hearts are not true, if our lives are hollow shells, it will not be enough. Our Lord will say, "I do not know you. Who are you? I never met you; depart from me."

So we need to pray that we will continue each day to say, "Lord, Lord," especially, "Lord Jesus Christ, son of God, have mercy on me, a sinner." Let us pray that we will not be people who talk a lot about the Lord but do not act according to his will. We should talk about the Lord, think about the Lord, read the words of the Lord, but then say "Lord Jesus Christ, son of God, have mercy on me, a sinner. Help my life to be transformed, so that I do what I say, and so that I am what I say." This requires God's grace and our own repentance.

So let's have a little time of examination of conscience as we reflect on these words of our Lord, and ask that God may bring our lives more into harmony with our lips.

> *Not every one who says to me, "Lord, Lord," shall enter the kingdom of heaven, but he who does the will of my Father who is in heaven. On that day many will say to me, "Lord, Lord, did we not prophesy in your name, and cast out demons in your name, and do many mighty works in your name?" And then will I declare to them, "I never knew you; depart from me, you evildoers."*

> *Every one then who hears these words of mine and does them will be like a wise man who built his house upon the rock; and the rain fell, and the floods came, and the winds blew and beat upon that house, but it did not fall, because it had been founded on the rock. And every one who hears these words of mine and does not do them will be like a foolish man who built his house upon the sand; and the rain fell, and the floods came, and the winds blew and beat against that house, and it fell; and great was the fall of it.*

With this, our Lord ends the Sermon on the Mount. He says: "Be like the wise man. Hear these words of mine and do them. Receive the Gospel of Christ, whose herald you now are. Believe what you read, teach what you believe, and practice what you teach." We may find it pleasant to hear the words of Jesus, to repeat the words of Jesus, to memorize them, to know them backwards and forwards, and yet we may be seeing them always at a distance. The words might be in the head and on the lips, but not in the heart, and rarely in the hands. Our Lord calls us to be people of integrity, to be clear all the way through. As he says earlier, the good tree bears good fruit, and the bad tree bears bad fruit. Purity of heart is to will one thing: we must be single minded. We must love the Lord our God with heart and mind and soul, and not merely with lips and intentions.

We admit that it is pleasant to be religious in a sort of superficial way. We can spend our life that way, and have a warm illusion of something valuable. But our Lord calls us to more than that. In these words in the Sermon on the Mount and in everything he says to us, he asks us to be engaged, to be totally committed, to live life seriously—to be, and not just to speak. I heard once of a spiritual writer who had been to Mass many times in her life. This person was a typical faithful Catholic in perhaps too superficial a way. And then, she wrote, once she went to Mass, and as a thousand times before, she said "I believe in God the Father Almighty, Creator of heaven and earth." She stopped and said, "Do I?" Does my life show that? A good point for us all to consider.

The Lord says, "Everyone then who hears these words of mine and does them will be like a wise man who built his house upon the rock. And the rain fell, and the floods came, and the winds blew and beat upon that house, but it did not fall, because it had been founded on the rock." My own Catholic community in Toronto has come a long way since its first bishop, Michael Power, built the cathedral. He listened to these words of Jesus. He talked about helping people, and then he decided to turn his words into action. Irish immigrants, refugees from the potato famine, were arriving in the city in the summer of 1847. He went down to the fever sheds where so many of them were dying of disease. While he was helping them, he caught their disease, and he died on October 1 of that same year. He heard, he spoke, but then he took action.

As Christians, we don't have the same obstacles faced by the early immigrants and the early Church. Do we have the fire? Do we have cohesive, simple, clear obedience to the will of the Lord? Or have we simply become co-opted into society, and have lost the fire? We are always in danger of losing the fire, because we're all sinners. But the Lord speaks to us now, as he spoke to those first disciples, and his words are a challenge to us. We can easily be comfortable Catholics, doing rather well in our modern society, and so we need to listen all the more to these words of our Savior when he says, "Everyone then who hears these words of mine and does them will be like a wise man who built his house upon a rock." Like the great saints, like the first bishop of Toronto, like the religious sisters who also came to help those who were dying, and gave their lives for them, we need to live out the words of Christ. "Every one then who hears these words of mine and does them will be like a wise man who built his house upon the rock; and the rain fell, and the floods came, and the winds blew and beat upon that house."

The rains always will fall and the winds will beat against us. We don't get a free ticket to heaven. Every generation has its challenges; every individual has his or her own personal challenges. Thomas More said to his son-in-law, "Master

Roper, we cannot expect to go to heaven on feather beds."
So let us listen to our Lord. The rain will fall, the floods will
come, the winds will blow and fall upon that house, but it
will not fall because it has been founded on the rock of integrity in both hearing and keeping the word of God. Receive
the Gospel of Christ, for we are all the heralds of that Gospel. Believe what we read—that is the first step. Believe what
we read, teach what we believe, and practice what we teach.
Because "everyone who hears these words of mine and does
not do them will be like a foolish man who built his house
upon the sand." The foolish man hoped nothing bad would
ever happen. But his house fell, and great was the fall of it.

Let us do a little checkup on the foundations now in our
own lives. Not too much—they say that when it comes to
guilt trips, Catholics are frequent fliers. But let's make a good
solid examination of conscience now, checking to see if there
are any cracks in the foundation, asking: "How often do I
build my life on 'Lord, Lord,' but do not do what he says?"
And let's ask the Lord now to help us to be people of integrity, who hear, read, listen, but then act, so that there is not a
wall between what we say and who we are and what we do.

> *Every one then who hears these words of mine
> and does them will be like a wise man who built
> his house upon the rock; and the rain fell, and the
> floods came, and the winds blew and beat upon
> that house, but it did not fall, because it had
> been founded on the rock. And every one who
> hears these words of mine and does not do them
> will be like a foolish man who built his house
> upon the sand; and the rain fell, and the floods
> came, and the winds blew and beat against that
> house, and it fell; and great was the fall of it.*

꠳

And when Jesus finished these sayings, the crowds were astonished at his teaching, for he taught them as one who had authority, and not as their scribes.

Much of the content of what Jesus teaches in the Sermon on the Mount is what the Jewish scribes were teaching. A lot of it is from the Old Testament. The content would probably have been familiar to the people listening. The difference here is the encounter with Christ—not just the content, but who is saying it. Our faith is not just the memorizing of a message; our faith is the encounter with our Savior. He is our Lord and our God, he who speaks as no one else speaks, who touches our hearts, and who can calm the sea. Because he spoke with authority, they were astonished. His authority is why we call him our Lord. Maybe we need to think about how often we say "Lord, Lord," and do not recognize that we should say, "My Lord and my God" with our lips, and mean it with our hearts, and prove it with our hands. We live our life in harmony with his Gospel, because of what the Gospel says, but also because of who says it. Praise to you, Lord Jesus Christ. Living out the words we hear is the way we receive the Gospel of the Lord, and that is the way we receive this great gift of the Sermon on the Mount. Let us pray it, and read it, and let it enter deep into our hearts.

꠳

Please reread the scripture passage at the beginning of the chapter (pages 126–127).

Our Father
Hail Mary
Glory Be

Born and raised in Guelph, Ontario, Archbishop Thomas Collins was ordained a priest in 1973. Collins considered other paths, but was inspired by a high school English teacher who suggested he should consider the priesthood. He obtained undergraduate and master's degrees in English, but later pursued theological training in Rome—where he specialized in the book of Revelation—while earning his licentiate in sacred scripture from the Pontifical Bible Institute. Collins earned a doctorate in theology from Gregorian University and was named bishop of St. Paul, Alberta, in 1997 and archbishop of Edmonton in 1999. Pope Benedict XVI appointed Collins the tenth archbishop of Toronto in December 2006.